A Vietı

MW01226041

My two tours to Vietnam with the Brown Water and Blue-Water Navy

Tom Johnson

RMCS (SW) USN (Ret)

USS Jennings County LST 846

Mekong Delta Riverine Patrol Force

USS Stribling DD-867

Yankee Station Tonkin Gulf

1967-1969

4

Note to Readers

I wrote this book more for personal reasons than anything else and wish I had done so many years ago when I could still remember events and names more clearly. The lack of notes, or a journal, to reference has left me at the mercy of my memory, and from almost 50 years down the road that memory does not provide the detail I wish it could. I have suffered from a lifetime of an inability to remember names of people though my memory of other details seems to stick around. I do name those I remember, or had access to information such as the cruise book I had for the USS Stribling's 1969 Tonkin Gulf deployment. I hope that the few I do recall are correct if not I apologize for the inaccuracies

I also write it as a personal recollection only, just my little piece of the story of Vietnam, and it is not intended in any way to be a definitive account of operations in the Delta or factually accurate for that matter though I did some research online to try to keep my facts as accurate as I could. Please take this in to account if you find inaccuracies or mistakes as I did not make them intentionally. I also apologize for any grammatical, spelling or formatting errors as I am a novice writer and did not have the book professionally edited.

Introduction

I start this recollection from the beginning of my first enlistment in the United States Navy and end it after my last deployment to Vietnam. I would serve a tour with the Riverine Patrol Force, in-country, deployed aboard the LST USS Jennings County, LST 846, in the Mekong Delta with Task Force 116, also known as the Brown Water Navy. I would return for another tour, this time to the Tonkin Gulf on an extended deployment, with the blue-water Navy serving aboard the Destroyer USS Stribling DD-867 which was deployed from the east coast of Florida out of her homeport of Mayport

These tours may not be considered front line combat tours but like thousands of other sailors, and the ships they served on, they provided valuable combat support services to front-line units such as the Riverine forces in the Mekong Delta and in the Tonkin Gulf to Navy Aircraft Carriers providing plane guard duties and protection on Yankee Station. They also served on the "Gun-line" providing gunfire support for ground combat units inland from the coast.

The danger was always present and there was no front line in the Delta, and no rear for that matter, everywhere was a combat zone. The Brown water and blue water ships did suffer combat and other casualties throughout the war during operations and I include comments on some of these incidents that happened while I was on my tours.

I deliberately did not read anything about the Vietnam War because I felt the politics of the war eclipsed what happened to the veterans. The politics were irrelevant to what this memorial was.

Maya Lin

Designer of the Vietnam Veterans Memorial

Acknowledgements

The photographs used in this book are from various online sources with the majority from Navsource.org and from the USS Stribling cruise book. I try to acknowledge the website and/or the person who took the photograph (if available).

The War Generations

The century I was born in, the twentieth century, seemed to have a war or conflict for every generation that came along. My Grandparents had WWI and my parents WWII, some of my older cousins had both WWII and Korea, my generation had Vietnam and my children's generation continued the trend with Desert Storm.

One of my earliest memories relates to war, it was of my mother and a neighbor talking over our front yard fence about bombing in Korea. I remember it mostly because with our neighbor's heavy southern accent she pronounced it 'bumming' instead of bombing, funny how something like that can stick in your head. I also remember hearing teachers at school discussing Korea as they watched us children play on the school playground during recess.

My father was too old and had too many children to serve in the military during WWII but, in a way, he did his part working as a firefighter at the Air Corps training base in Perry Florida.

The father of a neighborhood childhood friend served in WWII in the Navy and had brought home Japanese money, or Yen, from his tour in the Pacific. Occasionally my friend and I would take some Yen out the closet and play with it. The Yen was paper bills and small, about the same size as monopoly money which is exactly how we treated it.

The most I ever heard my friend's father mention about his service was that he was an Engineman Third Class on a ship in the Pacific. He loved to watch Victory at Sea and would always whistle to imitate the sound of a bomb dropping from planes.

Two of my oldest cousins served in the Pacific, one on my mother's side and one on my father's. My mother's nephew was stationed at Schofield Barracks Hawaii when it was bombed by the Japanese on December 7, 1942. I remember an article written in the local newspaper where he related how he and other soldiers stationed at Schofield Barracks used anything they had at hand to fire at the Japanese planes as they attacked the base including 45 caliber pistols.

Another older cousin on my father's side had been in the thick of it in the Pacific and had brought home a machine gun as a souvenir. How he managed that I don't know and whether it was actually a Japanese machine gun I don't know either, but suspect it was. Anyway, I can remember seeing it in a closet at his house and everyone in the family knew what it was and as I grew up with his two sons, who were close to my age, we would now and then look at the machine gun, but my older cousin never spoke about the gun or the war.

A third member of my family, a step cousin, was in the early combat action in South Korea when the North Korean Army attacked his entire unit was captured during this initial surge and my cousin spent the rest of the war as a Prisoner of War. At times the local newspaper would reprint the photo of his return home with many of the family standing in a group around him welcoming his return, including my Mother and oldest Brother. During his POW years he kept a running list of names of men that died in the camp which he turned in when he was freed from captivity. He had written these names in tiny letters on a piece of paper which he wrapped inside the casing of a fountain pen.

All around me were these living generations of the Second World War and the Korean conflict, but these veterans said little about their time during these wars. They home settled down, went back to work, got married and began raising the next generation, a generation that would become known as the baby

11

boomer generation. On November 6, 1946 I entered this world as part of that generation.

WWII defined what was to come after the war as far as subsequent conflicts like Korea and Vietnam. Korea has its own muddled history and Vietnam had been under French control until the Japanese took over after Germany defeated the French. After the war the French returned, but not for long. An insurgency called the Viet Minh, led by a communist by the name of Ho Chi Minh, who had fought a guerilla war against the Japanese, took control of Hanoi declaring independence from France citing the words from the American Declaration of Independence that "all men are created equal". He would defeat the French, but that was not the end of it because the United States had concluded that the expansion of communism in South East Asia was one of the gravest threats to America, and to Democracy that then existed. Now it was our turn to take on Mr. Ho Chi Minh.

So, I had all this war legacy surrounding me as I was growing up and had no doubt that, one day, I too would serve in the military, the draft would make sure of that, but for the period from my birth until I was eighteen it was just the process of growing up that occupied my life. I was fortunate to have a working father and a stay at home mother, and though we were not exactly middle class, we had a good home and food on the table and decent clothes to wear. The neighborhood I grew up in was a less well-to-do section of town but was an area that had contributed many to the wars of the Twentieth Century, and would do the same for Vietnam.

There were no college exemptions for most of those in my neighborhood, not many could afford, or even thought about, going to college and most parents just hoped they could get all their kids through high school which they themselves most likely never attended themselves as many rural schools in North Florida prior to World War II only taught to either the sixth or the eighth grades. My father grew up on a farm and completed his schooling at the sixth grade and my mother who grew up living in various logging camps completed her education at the eighth grade level.

I'm sure it was a disappointment for them when I dropped out in my senior year to join the Navy. I would finish with a GED later on but to be so close and not finish was really dumb on my part and I always felt I let my mother down when I did leave school. At the time though I had been in school for 14 years having been held back twice from missing too many days because of child hood asthma. Finally I decided it was enough and left, I was a half credit shy of a diploma.

I didn't think much about military duty until I was out of school, as I already mentioned I was too busy growing up to think too much about it, however it was a topic at times amongst us "draft eligible teens" especially as our school days grew shorter. My neighborhood buddy decided to take a chance with the draft, against my advice, I told him he would wind up in the jungles of Vietnam. Turned out the roles got reversed, he went to Korea as an Army mechanic and I went to Vietnam, though not quite to the jungle I had envisioned for my buddy.

Finally facing the reality of either being drafted or joining I joined the United States Navy on October 7, 1965. I received my draft notice two weeks in to boot camp. That was close.

I had joined the Navy because it had been a dream of mine since I was about the age of nine when my older brother joined, which was in 1956. It was a big deal to our family as he was the first to go in to the military. As I stood at the edge of the front porch watching him leave in a big gray Navy van, I believe that it was right then and there I decided to do the same when I was old enough. I'm not sure if it was because I wanted to follow in my older brothers' footsteps or that I wanted to ride in a big Navy Van, at nine years old you can have screwy priorities.

And for the life of me I couldn't figure out why mama was so upset, sitting in a rocking chair crying, to me it was an exciting day.

Well I did join, but there was no big Grey Navy van coming to the house to pick me up, or mama crying, unless she did so after I left the house. My daddy and I walked the mile to town where I was picked up at the Post Office by the Recruiter and taken to the bus station, and I was on my way to Boot Camp.

Basic Training
Great Lakes, IL

October 1965

To back up a little, before getting on that bus, I had taken the recruit exam at the Perry Florida Post Office which had been built in 1930 by the WPA the Work Progress Administration that was putting Americans back to work during the depression. The Recruiter had his office down a hallway on one side past the rows of mailboxes on the wall. The Recruiter, a First Class Petty Office dressed in Navy summer whites impressed me with how sharp he looked in the white uniform. He was nice and friendly as he administered the exam. I would soon learn that not all Navy First Class Petty Officers were that nice.

Also taking the test that day were two boys I knew from High School who would be in my boot camp company. We all passed the exam and told to come back the next day for the trip to Jacksonville, Florida for processing into the Navy. The ride to Jacksonville, Florida was by Greyhound Bus where we spent the night in a Hotel somewhere in town. The next day we were taken to the Naval Air Station for the induction process.

After arriving at the processing center, along with a busload of other recruits, I found myself in a blur of activity as I was run through a series of filling out of forms, and then on to a fast and furious physical exam (my first encounter with the term *bend over and grab your ankles*). After being sworn in as a group by a Navy officer we boarded another bus for the trip to the Jacksonville airport. I don't remember eating during the processing time but I'm sure we did at some point, but it was such a rushed time I can't remember what we ate or where we ate it.

I had been with my two high school friends at the beginning but became separated during the processing at some point and I'm not sure when I saw them again, probably on the plane. However, I do remember boarding the plane and being seated on the aisle seat. Somehow I was able to exchange to the window seat but lack any memory of the details of how the seat swap came about though I remember a flight Stewardess was involved (and yes, that's what they were called back then, Stewardess's). It was to be my first plane ride, and I was excited about that. I still have a memory of my face being glued to the window until we arrived at Chicago O'Hare International airport. I remember that the lights of the city seemed to spread out for miles when looking out the window as the plane circled in a holding pattern for a while before landing. I had never seen anything like it.

After landing at O'Hare we had to wait for further transportation to the Great Lakes Navy Training Center, located about 15 miles from North Chicago. We finally boarded a bus and were taken to the base. We offloaded at the gate and ordered to line up. I remember that taps were playing as we did this. We were finally marched, well walked, to a section of the center called Camp Barry where we were deposited in a red brick building, circa 1904 vintage.

The training center had existed since prior to WWI and was originally authorized to be built by the Theodore Roosevelt administration in 1904. The original red brick buildings built during that time were still being used at Camp Barry when I arrived and it was my first of many barracks I would be privileged to stay in over the years. They didn't look all that bad and most likely had been upgraded periodically, but a bunk is bunk no matter how old the building and we were happy to see it and finally were able to go to bed sometime around midnight.

We didn't see the bunks for long. At five in the morning the yelling started. Bleary eyed and confused I dressed and

16

hustled with the rest outside to form a line. We were assaulted with a continuous stream of yelling and orders to close up and "Move it!" Somehow we wound up at a chow hall where the yelling continued unabated as we stood in line. Memory is hazy here, I guess I ate but not sure if I was awake enough to remember what I ate, or to care for that matter.

The next couple of days were spent being issued our uniforms, underwear, socks, a seabag and other odds and ends, then having our hair cut completely off with the traditional buzz cut. We spent time stenciling uniforms and learning the rudiments of running helter-skelter everywhere we went, called double time. Recruits were not allowed to walk at any time they were outside the barracks. Oh, we also had another physical (*bend over and grab your ankles*). All the while the yelling never ceased.

We were yelled at by upper recruits on their service week duties as we stood in line at the chow hall. We were crunched close together by the yelling upper boots telling us to get nuts to butts. No matter how close you got to the guy in front of you they were never satisfied screaming in your ear *"I said nuts to butts boot!"*

The food was decent, mostly, different for me than what I had been used to eating at home. We ate a lot of beans and greens in the south but the chow line had enough of the same kinds of food I was ok. Even with the different, and new foods to me, I ate well and would wind up gaining weight and adding muscle during my boot time. Breakfast was my favorite meal, and always had been, and the Navy breakfast was about as good as it could get, and I enjoyed the food. For the noon and evening meals you could always count on the Navy to have mashed potatoes at least one meal and rice at another, along with whatever meat was being served that day so it was food I could adapt to but not cooked like my Mamas for sure.

The fun really started when we moved to a second location into barracks that were slightly more modern, at least not quite the vintage of the old brick barracks, these were old WWII barracks built in the H pattern, two end buildings that housed the bunk dormitories and the connecting middle section with showers and heads. The buildings were two stories and my company had the right side upstairs dorm. They were of the typical barn style with bunks close together in rows. At least we had advanced one war in living conditions.

We began drilling in earnest at this location. When we were not out on the grinder (parade ground) practicing formations and marching we were in various class's that covered different aspects of Navy and shipboard life. I don't recall a lot of detail of the classes but the marching and drilling sticks with me. I did get busted for dozing off in one class by First Class who was droning on about his service during the Korean War.

I liked the marching once we got the hang of it. We began looking more like a marching company instead of a bunch of wild turkeys trying to march in formation. You could tell the difference in the progress of the various companies as they advanced through training. On the march to the chow hall the more advanced companies where in the lead and were sharp looking and well-practiced in their turns and marching steps. This became less so as the other companies who had been in training for a shorter period approached the chow hall. The last in line were the "boots" who showed little of the tight, precision marching of the older more practiced company formations.

My own company was a sloppy comical looking new boot company that first week. Then we began to get it together gaining snap to our steps and improving on the clock like turns as we practiced on the parade ground, or Grinder, We sharply

18

followed the barked orders company recruit leader as we followed behind the Guide-on (the fellow who carried the company flag on a pole at the front of the formation). We soon became proud of our precision and I enjoyed the marching. I would later join a drill team during my A school period and would enjoy that as well.

Another thing we spend a good deal of time on was the 16-count manual which was the various positions of the rifle through a routine of shouldering, presenting and otherwise doing parade ground stuff all in the name of military discipline.

Something I never had to worry about at home because my mother took care of was washing clothes. One of the first things we were taught after moving to the new location was hand washing our clothes and hanging them in a drying room to dry (it was October and beginning to get nippy in Great Lakes). The only demerit I received while in training was for hanging my watch sweater inside out. I had to do an hour of extra duty to work it off and this extra duty was in one of the big hanger like buildings where we had to do various exercises for a solid hour with no break. The one that sticks with me is one where you had to rest the Springfield rifle, which was a heavy rifle, across your ankles while flat on your back and do leg lifts. It was easy until about the 3rd one, then "Oh boy" did that rifle gain weight.

We moved to our third, and newest, barracks at the training center after two or three weeks at the WWII dorm barracks. The dorm part was the same but the distance between bunks increased were a little bigger. There was more locker space, and a nicer lounge that we only saw in the evenings just before taps.

It was at this time we were informed by our Company Commander that we would be moving to an accelerated training schedule due to the increase of recruits coming in for the Vietnam build up. We would now graduate basic in nine weeks instead of 12.

For the next eight weeks it was nothing but go, go and more go. Along with the physical training activities we also went to different classes in seamanship, firefighting school, and took part in competitions with other units for coveted flags for different events. I think we wound up with three flags we won. As we became better at marching and dressing ranks and keeping our uniforms sharp looking we gained confidence and it showed in our marching. The other companies were feeling the same, and it was obvious from the fine marching formations that were on display every evening as we marched to the chow hall. I remember there was a building we marched by where visitors could watch as we marched by and all the companies would really lay it on as we went by.

As our company advanced nearer to the front each week we became like the sharp looking companies we so admired during our first week in training, no longer resembling the awkward chicken leg marching formation we exhibited at the start of our training. Some of the more musically talented boys learned to sing marching cadences that were sung sing-song fashion to time our march step. They became good at it, keeping us in precision step as we marched along. One in particular was good at it, a short redheaded guy full of spunk and sharp as hell in his marching. Everybody liked him and he wound up being one of the best cadence callers and was our guide on flag bearer for the company. He's the short guy at front on the left in the company picture as we marched at graduation.

We were proud and had toughened up in the weeks of training and no longer felt like boots; we now felt like United States Navy Sailors and took pride in our new roles. There was less yelling and straighter talk from the Company Commander and the other Petty Officers we dealt with now and this let us know we were getting there, heading towards the end.

The last two weeks of boot camp were the easiest but still busy. We went to see our career counselor and filled out our request for orders. I wanted an A school right out of boot camp but then couldn't decide which one to try for. The counselor, on finding out I had a brother stationed in Key West, advised that I could ask for brother duty for a year (in Navy terminology DUBRO) spend a year stationed near him then apply for school. This is what I opted for and it was a good thing I did because I had no clue what to do and I needed an older person's guidance.

We graduated from Great Lakes after nine weeks and the ceremony was held in a huge hanger style building. The site of all the sharp looking companies with their many flags flying, marching one after the other was breathtaking. My company was in the early ones in the marching order so, I got to see other company's marching in and it was thrilling what with the martial music. After all the companies were inside the building, and facing the grandstand with its assembled brass, there were speeches and congratulations and then it was over. We were no longer Recruits having been automatically advanced on graduation from E-1 Seaman Recruit to E-2 Seaman Apprentice.

I'm in there some place, we were a proud bunch that day

We had packed and been ready to go after the ceremony and left almost immediately for the airport on a Navy bus. When we headed out the gate the fellow who had been the primary cadence caller started the chants on the bus, but this time he used the vulgar lyrics instead of the ones allowed during "official" marches, I won't repeat the words he used here but still remember them. He was a short feisty red head who had also been the guide-on for the company and well-liked by the entire company.

At the airport, after I had ate at one of the restaurants located in the terminal, I paid a visit to the men's room and the Navy uniform being of the old traditional button up flap design with no pockets the standard place to carry a wallet of the folding type was to hook it in the waistband of the trousers under the cover of the Jumper blouse so it would not be seen. To take down the pants, you had to remove the wallet and unbutton the flap to do your business. Well I laid the wallet on the floor after unbuttoning, proceeded to do my business and left the bathroom after finishing. It was about 30 minutes later that I discovered I was missing my wallet. In a panic I rushed back to the stall I had used, but the wallet was gone. It was a blow as it had all the money I had for the entire boot period. Now I was flat broke, had lost my ID card and hadn't even made it to my first assignment. Luckily, I had my manila packet with my orders and records.

Not a good start to my Navy career.

Key West Florida
1965-1966

After a two week leave period at home, my brother Wayne came up to Perry from Key West to meet me and we rode back to Key West on a Greyhound bus, it was one long ride and I mostly napped. We swapped buses at Miami and I remember when I got off the bus how nice and tropical the weather felt like as when we had left Perry in North Florida it was cold enough to wear jackets but in south Florida it was summer whites weather and I was in Navy Wool Blues.

I won't go in to any detail about my year in Key West as there was nothing exciting about the time I spent stationed there other than I did a bit of growing up. I was attached to the Key West Test and Evaluation Detachment or KEYWESTEVDET whose primary mission was to test and evaluate torpedoes, mines and other weapons. I was eventually assigned to one of the small boats used to take the various weaponry out to sea for testing but the boat I was on spent most the time out of the water being worked on. I think me, and the one other lower crewman, chipped and painted every inch, several times.

I started catching rides up to North Florida with some other sailors from the North Florida area and we split the cost of gas with the guy who owned the car. It was a long trip but helped ease the homesickness I had continued to feel since joining the Navy. We probably went once a month or so. I was always broke as all my paycheck pretty much went for these trips. My Navy paycheck of $47 every two weeks ($58 after I made seaman) did not stretch far. At first we didn't receive checks, on paydays we stood in line at the Navy Exchange Cafeteria with a form that we filled out called a Pay Chit which we handed to the pay clerk who matched it against a name on a list and you received cash money. I don't remember when we did receive checks but sometime early on we did.

With my brother's much needed guidance during my year at Key Wes and at his encouragement I applied and received orders to the Radioman Class A school at Bainbridge Maryland with a prerequisite school for and eight-week Basic Electricity and Electronics that was located at my Basic Training location, Great Lakes Training Center, but this time I was going there as a student and not a boot. My brother Wayne was a Radioman First Class at the time I was stationed with him and had been in the navy for 10 years. He had achieved his Radioman rating the hard way by doing what was known as striking for the rate, basically working on the job (OJT) while he studied the course material on his own. He was instrumental in my going to the Radioman A school and after my year in Key West doing not much of anything useful other than either applying paint on to something or chipping paint off something I was finally on a course to learning something of a more professional nature, even though, as I would find out later, I was not completely done with applying paint or removing it.

I was not unhappy to see my last of Key West though I would return several times in later years, but only for short visits. I would spend Christmas at home in Perry and then head for my school at the Naval Training Command Great Lakes, Illinois.

Basic Electronics and Electricity
NTC Great Lakes

January–March 1967

Well, I was back in Great Lakes, scene of my Boot Camp days, but this time it was a little different and I don't mean because there were piles of snow everywhere and had not been when I left Boot Camp but different in that I was coming back for a good technical school, eight weeks long, and I was a seaman with one year and a couple of months of Navy time under my belt. Not exactly an old salt, but no longer a tenderfoot, or "Boot" in Navy lingo.

In the area of the training center I was attending school I saw none of the boot camp activities I had experienced, and I didn't miss seeing it either. We had regimentation at the School and had to conform to what were called *"Mickey Mouse rules"* but otherwise it was not a bad time there. No marching back and forth to class as I would have to do in the Radioman A school portion of the training later, but at Great Lakes the barracks life was more relaxed.

We lived in the open bay barn type barracks built during World War Two (the exact same layout as my second barracks in boot camp), and the small 2x6 bunks were only a few feet apart. We had decent lockers and the bathrooms (heads) were clean (cleaned by, guess who? The students). I bunked close to two guys who were in the advanced Electronics Technician School and became friends with them during the time I was there, and they would later do me a great service by helping me with my math.

The big downside of my time at BEEP school was the constant snowing and piles of snow everywhere. It kept us cooped up in the barracks at night and on the weekends, which was probably good for me as it inclined me to study more and I needed that.

The one memorable thing I recall is I received my first income tax check while there with Thomas B Johnson on the front and before I could cash it found out it was a different Thomas B Johnson because I received a second IRS check a day later. There was a different SSN, so I kept mine and mailed the other one back, hope the guy got it.

Let me say a little more about the snow. Being from Florida this was new territory for me as I had only experienced snow only once before when I was twelve years old and it snowed in North Florida, three whole inches. It was a fun snow and melted quickly. I had arrived at Great Lakes in early January and it was cold and there was a lot of snow on the ground.

The next day after I arrived was Saturday and the barracks Master at Arms assigned me to duty chopping ice off the sidewalks around the barracks. The tool was a straight flat bladed device with a handle, like a flattened out hoe. You used it by chopping up the ice into small pieces and then scraping them to the side. After about three steps I slipped and fell tearing a gash in my uniform pants and bruising my thigh. Luckily it was just the uniform, and I only had a sore hip for a while, but a lesson learned about ice and snow. I was on my way to adjusting on how to walk on ice, and with dealing with what seemed like tons of snow.

By February the snow was piled so high on the sides of the sidewalks that ran between the barracks it was like walking through a deep trench or a tunnel with no top, something I imagined the WWI trenches would have been like with snow instead of dirt. It was always cold there, but the barracks were always toasty and warm. Students only had short walks to the various places they needed to go such as the Chow hall, barracks and school so, we stayed warm in our wool blues and heavy pea coat jackets. But still, it was polar opposites from what I had been used to as a native of Florida and spending the past year in what was pretty much the tropics of Key West.

The daily routine at the school was class all day, a smoke break in the morning and afternoon, lunch break and barracks duty about once a week when the duty crew would clean heads and rotate a barracks watch at night. The first day we were issued a wooden square box about double the size of a shoe box that contained several items, a breadboard (had connector holes for electronic circuit building and testing practice circuits), a Simmons Multimeter (big, about 5x7x4), various electronic components for the practice circuits and a slide rule which I knew existed, but had no clue how to use but would soon learn enough to use it for what I needed during the school.

We had to take a round of tests to determine our placement in one of three class levels, depending on how you scored dictated which one you would be assigned to. There were 8 weeks 6 and 4-week classes, the four week being the accelerated class. I didn't do well enough on the test for higher levels so was placed in the 8-week course as were most of the students.

Students that had strong math skills and had previous background in electronics were assigned to the more advanced classes. Along with being assigned to the lowest level class it was determined I would have to attend night math school to bring my math skills up to a level that would allow me to complete the course. If I didn't pass the night math class, I would be dropped. Math, to me, had always been so boring that I could generate no interest in it during high school happily accepting a D grade as something good. Now I would pay for that laziness.

The classroom was arranged in a horseshoe pattern with tables around the edges of the room and the instructor seated at

28

the open end at the head of the class where a blackboard was located. I found out fast that Navy instructors don't waste a lot of time on preliminaries and tended to dive right in to the subject matter. Before I knew it I was learning all about electrical and electronics basics, it was both fun and demanding.

The night math class was an additional burden on me, and I was regretting my lack of interest in high school. I was considering the consequences of being dropped from the school and feeling doomed before even starting the math class.

Surprisingly I did well in the beginning as we went through standard math, the adding, subtracting, multiplying and fractions. Then we got in to Algebra and it was like a brick wall. No matter how hard I tried, I just couldn't get this strange form of math. I about at the end of my rope when one night my two barracks mates from the advanced Electronics Technician School came through the TV break room and saw me and while talking I told them about my problem, I explained I had never taken algebra in high school and having a hard time learning the transposing part which was just plain baffling to me.

The two set down and began working with me. These two guys stuck with me over the next several nights showing me different ways to work problems and then one night it clicked. I mean, I got it! After that I practically breezed through the night course having no further problems even when they threw in the calculus and trigonometry. I never forgot how those two guys, their names long lost to my memory, took the time to help me at my lowest point during the school, and they never considered it a big deal, they were just helping out a barracks mate.

After eight weeks of Basic Electronics and Electricity school I graduated, considerably smarter about electronics than I ever thought I would be, but I still had another 18 weeks of training ahead of me. So, I was off to Radioman A School.

Radioman Class A School
NTC Bainbridge Maryland

March to June 1967

Naval Training Center Bainbridge established in 1941 as a recruit training base had previously been a boy's school. After the war Bainbridge NTC was deactivated, but then reopened to train sailors in various ratings one being the Radioman Class A school. When I arrived there, the weather was in March the weather was turning nice, and that was a good thing because unlike at the Basic Electronics School at Bainbridge we had to march back and forth from our barracks to class daily and to the chow hall at lunch. The barracks were by now familiar, WWII wooden barracks style with no air conditioning and the barn dorm living areas. These WWII temporary structures certainly had lasting power.

We went to school five days a week for 8 hours and when we returned to our barracks, we had to hold field days on certain days and sometimes would have duty days which meant standing quarterdeck watches at various barracks.

I had stood enough duty days in Key West, and BEEP school that I started looking for a way out (referred to as skating out) and I found a way. Or at least I thought I had but, it wound up being more work than the duty days were. When my class fell in for our first march to school, I noticed that there was a sharp marching drill team at the head of the column of all classes.

The classes formed in order of oldest to newest class and the drill team led all the classes on our back-and-forth marches from school to barracks. The drill team looked super sharp and had these neat black and white braided cords wrapped over one arm shoulder. Boy did they impress me with their sharp marching and precision moves as we marched the route to school. I was hooked and resolved to join the team.

I applied after my second week, tried out and was accepted. The tradeoff for not having to stand duty, as I found out quick enough, was we had practice twice a week, after class, and we also had to travel to various locations in the area to march in parades, on weekends! Marching in the parades turned out to be enjoyable even though I was not particularly fond of all the bus traveling we had to do.

The practice I endured, and it was definitely necessary as we had to learn some fairly intricate maneuvers and only practice can make you perfect in that. Other things we had to do as drill team members was to rotate duty holding evening Retreat (the lowering of the flag while taps played). This was held at the headquarters building where a three-person team would lower the flag at sunset. It was less than half an hour and also enjoyable to me; I had found I liked the ceremonial stuff. The fun, and enjoyment, of being on an elite drill team was still better than standing barracks watches and spending Saturday's playing cards or watching television.

In many of the towns where we marched in parades the locals would go all out to express their appreciation. We would be invited in to their local taverns where they would buy us beers though most of us were not old enough to drink. The uniforms made us old enough to them. I had a great time on the drill team and it was worth all the work learning the various maneuvers and performance tricks that the parade audience loved, and who always gave us high praise for coming to their small towns to march. I don't recall ever running in to anyone who was not a nice person in these small towns, most of which were in eastern Pennsylvania area.

Drill Team or not I still had school to deal with. The course material was fast paced and covered a lot of subjects and, almost immediately, we began Morse code training. The first two weeks of code training consisted of learning a few characters a day and practicing them over and over with music playing in our headsets. This was not a bad way to learn I found out as the music was recent rock songs picked for the rhythm and the purpose was to train students to use a rhythm while copying the code. Surprisingly the music helped. Later we would do daily practice just to increase receiving skills and advance through the various speeds, I topped out at 22 wpm and was working on 24 when the class ended.

Other training covered a wide scope of electronics and radio communications, we picked up where we had ended in the electronics training from BE&E school moving in to Vacuum tube and transistor theory and learning circuit diagrams the super heterodyne radio circuit. We covered Radio Teletype along with radio wave propagation, message formatting and other items related to Navy Fleet Communications.

Classes were five days a week, and we marched to class, to lunch and to the barracks after class daily. After joining the drill team, I marched with it two or three times a week after school. The Drill team was the lead group to lead out and arrive at the school. All this marching, along with my drill duties and practice, caused me for years afterword to always have the impulse to get in step with anyone I happened to be walking with. My weekends were filled with Drill team events or, if not occupied with that, either hanging out at the barracks or going to the Fiddlers Green club to drink 3.2 near beer.

July saw the end of school and all my class graduated with no one washing out. I have a class photo from this period and for a while after graduating I remained in touch with a few of my classmates but, gradually, time and distance ended any contact with them. After almost 50 years I can't recall many of

32

their names but remember a lot of the faces. I think I graduated 19 out of 40 something and always thought I could have done much better but had, gradually, began partying more and studying less and this does tend to lower one's grades. But graduate I did and received my diploma and was ready for whatever came next, whatever it might be. I was soon to find out.

Orders to Vietnam
June 1967

After 24 weeks of school, including BEEP school, we were down to the last two weeks of classes at the Radioman A school. These two weeks were, almost, stress free compared to the previous 22. We went through a final round of reviewing course material and taking final exams. As one instructor liked to put it, the school course we just went through was the equivalent of a two-year junior college course crammed into a 26-week period.

It had been fast paced with a lot of material covered, but none one washed out and all in my class graduated. and became designated Radioman. We had earned our sparks, the four lightning bolts rating symbol that we wore on our shoulder sleeves, and now we were ready to head to the fleet and work real-world Navy communications.

I passed all written tests, and the code test. The 16 WPM test speed seemed slow after going up to 24 WPM during training and practice. All this Morse code training was deemed necessary as a backup communications method but would primarily be used for drill exercises as the Navy was transitioning to better and faster means of communications, mainly radio Teletype which we had also trained on during school. The CW drills did help me keep my proficiency in copying code and sending code, and in 1975 I was able to pass the 13wpm Amateur Radio Code test for my General Class Amateur Radio license. So, technically I became both a professional and an amateur radio operator.

The slowdown in the tempo of classwork enabled me and my classmates to enjoy those last two weeks as, usually, after we took our daily exam we could goof off in the parade area and smoke all we wanted or, would be let loose early and we would go back and hang out at the barracks taking it easy. The weather was gorgeous in Bainbridge at this time of the year and we would lie out on the grass in front of the barracks sunning, smoking and talking.

The rest of the world seemed distant to us this spring of 1967 even with all that was going on in the Middle East and South East Asia. A war between Israel and the Arab countries was just ending in what was to become known as the six days war and the U.S. was increasing the number of troops to Vietnam. But, none of this seemed to apply to us, not yet anyway. We were young enough to be heavily involved in listening to rock music and had become big fans of the hit TV series Star Trek. Much was going on in the Space Race as we seemed to launch space vehicles on a regular basis as the nation prepared for the trip to the moon before the end of the 1960s, the time frame that President Kennedy had set for the mission completion. It was a brief period, and we enjoyed it, but we also knew we would head out to the fleet and becoming part of some radio shack gang in distant parts of the world. We were expecting our orders to be posted any day.

The posting of the orders came as a list tacked on the bulletin board outside the Administrative office in the Radioman school building. I can remember all my classmates crowded around looking for their names and where they were going, some happy, some not. I read mine and was a little confused by the SGN that was listed after the ship I was being assigned to, the USS Jennings County LST-846. I asked one of the instructors, a First-Class Petty Officer, what the SGN stood for. He explained that the USS Jennings County along with several other WWII LST's were being used as patrol ships in the Mekong Delta. The SGN stood for Saigon. So, I was on my way to Vietnam but being young and not really expecting to be in any danger I did not spend much time thinking about the upcoming transfer since I was more excited about going home after graduating than I was about getting to my next duty station.

I had last seen my Family at Christmas 1966 and I was looking forward to spending some time at home. I would have a week there and then a few days with one of my sisters in California before flying on to Saigon and my first shipboard duty assignment, and my first trip outside the United States. This was my first foreign country I would visit. Little did I know it would not be my last.

While at home I ran into one of my childhood friends, a fellow by the name of Steve Smith. It would be the last time I would see him alive. He would join the Marine Corps and die in Vietnam. I will always remember him as the smiling friendly boy I knew from our childhood days.

Saigon
Republic of Vietnam

1967

Photo: Saigon Street view from a military bus

After my leave I flew out from Tallahassee, Florida to San Francisco leaving a few days early so I could spend some time with my sister in California. Afterwards I flew out of Travis AFB aboard a Tiger Airline charter plane headed for Saigon, Vietnam. It was a long flight and boring. We landed at Clark AFB in the Philippines for refueling and after landing we were notified there had been an engine problem of some sort so we would be there for a few hours.

I don't remember how long we waited but, finally, we started our final leg to Saigon. As we approached the city the flight attendant announced that we would be coming in at a steep decent in to the airport. Though they did not say so, I have always thought this was a maneuver to avoid any rocket fire.

The flight landed safely, and I got off with the other passengers and entered the terminal which, from what little I can remember, was not impressive but not rundown either. All passengers were directed to a barred window where we had to change all our U.S. money to Military Script, or MPC. After exchanging our greenbacks, we boarded a Navy Grey bus that would transport us to our temporary lodgings while we waited for further transport to our commands.

The most memorable thing I recall of my arrival in my first foreign country was the smell. A smell that was different from the smells I was used to in the U.S. It would become a smell I would associate with Vietnam the rest of my life. I can't describe it with my limited writing skills, but it was a tangy, earthy, spicy smell. It was a smell created from the tropical atmosphere along with various smells from, who knows what, of spices, clothes, vegetation, but boy it didn't smell like Florida, and it was strong! The weather did remind me of a Florida summer though.

Besides the smell the other thing that struck me were the buildings, packed close along the streets with lots of people moving about helter-skelter. Most of the buildings were ones that the French had built that looked like a turn of the century structures and not American in style at all. I guess it was more of the French Colonial look. The city atmosphere likely had something to do with the smell. Even down in the delta the smells were not the same as I was used to but different from what I had sniffed in Saigon. Eventually I got used to the smells and stopped noticing.

The bus deposited us at an old French Hotel that was being utilized by the Navy as transient quarters. There was not much to the rooms as I recall, and I think there were several of us to a room, more a cube than a room. The bathrooms and showers were in a central courtyard and you can imagine my surprise when I went to take a shower and found that at one end of the courtyard there were several women washing clothes by hand at a little fountain. They paid me no mind though and since we were not directly in their line of vision to I took my shower and there were other guys showering so it seemed to be the norm.

The place we went to eat was ran by the military and we had to purchase a book of tickets to use there, so within a few hours I had gone from American money to Military money to BX cafeteria money (or tickets). So, we traded some of our military script for the tickets and I think I mainly lived on Hamburgers while we were in Saigon since I have never been much for strange or different foods and had never even tried oriental food of any sort and I didn't eat my first fried rice until I was in Japan almost a year later.

The day after our arrival we were taken to the Navy Support Activity building in Saigon, not because they deemed us important enough to visit it but because they needed the walls in the hallways painted (the Navy will paint anything, over and over). It was not hard work and passed the time and I was no stranger to painting as I had already been indoctrinated in my year in Key West. The Headquarters building was near a main street lined with venders and we walked over to this street looking for something we could eat at lunch time but, again, I didn't see anything I liked. I don't remember what I did eat, and may have waited until that night when I could get a hamburger at the military cafeteria.

I remember the main street we visited also had the French Colonial look I had observed on the bus ride from the airport, and there were many vendors with little booths all along the sidewalks. The street was busy with cars, mopeds and bicycles and it was loud. The Vietnamese dress was mixed with some traditional looking oriental dress and some western, usually pants with a white shirt.

We returned to the building to finish our day of painting. Not exciting stuff but, hey it's the Navy if it don't move paint it.

One thing I failed to mention was that to enter, or leave, the building you had to walk between two machine gun positions, one on each side, manned by some very bored looking Vietnamese soldiers. I was still adjusting to all the guns I saw around the area, but no one seemed to be overly worried about an imminent attack as all the guards I saw looked relaxed.

This was posted on line as a view from the French Hotel that was used for temporary quarters for transient Navy personnel.

A Gooney Bird Flight
Tan San Nhut Air Base

About our third day in Saigon we were told to get our gear ready and boarded a bus to Tan San Nhut Air Base. We arrived and were sent out to board an old C-47 Dakota airplane, lovingly referred to as a Gooney Bird; this was a twin-engine propeller plane that was used to haul cargo and passengers around in Vietnam. The planes were flown by contractors who did not have to adhere to the military dress standard and our pilot was living proof of that. There was about six of us and we were told to stand down on the runway due to some engine repairs that were ongoing with the plane. So, we sat in the hot sun, on a concrete runway and waited. One fellow had a bottle of booze and passed it around, but I didn't drink being afraid I would throw up what with the heat. Eventually they boarded us, and we had to sit on canvas sling seats along the sides (like the old WWII paratroopers in the movies) with cargo and mail sacks in the middle of the plane. As we sat, there waiting to take off a rough looking, semi-bald-headed man steeped out of the cockpit, he was wearing a dirty stained undershirt, had about a three-day growth of whiskers and was holding a coffee cup. He slowly looked around the plane as though he was evaluating if the plane would make it off the ground with all the stuff piled in the middle and then crossed himself with his hand, turned and returned to the cockpit. It was either a scare tactic intended as a joke or he was serious and to this day I don't know which but at the time it had the effect of scaring the crap out of me intended or not.

We took off and everything went smooth as we landed at one place, offloaded and on-loaded cargo. We finally came in to our destination which was the Vietnamese Navy base at Vung Tao. We made a wheel's touchdown but then the pilot gunned the plane and went around and landed. Not sure why he did so but one of the other guys on the plane said he missed the runway. When we debarked from the plane I saw that the runway was the metal grid stuff they used for combat air fields and not concrete. I mean this was WWII stuff like the CB's laid down on the islands that were captured in the Pacific.

I never had the opportunity to ride another Gooney Bird, and I am very thankful for that, but they did have a reputation of continuing to fly under almost any circumstances and were extremely reliable, a true workhorse of war.

Vung Tao
RVN Navy Base

Vung Tao Vietnamese Navy Base is located on a peninsula that juts out in to the South China Sea but angles almost parallel to the Vietnamese coast. This was a way station on our route to the mouth of the Bassac River where we would meet our ride to the Jennings County but before I continue with that journey I will describe the base and what I did there while waiting on transport down the coast.

Vietnamese Village near Vung Tao Vietnamese Navy Base

During our several days stay at the base we were assigned various odd jobs, one of which was digging a ditch for a water line for a CB group at the base. It was hot work. My fellow traveler, and A school classmate, who had been with me the whole time on this trip was from New York City. He had been a bank worker prior to joining the Navy had fair skin and blond hair, and after a few hours of working in the heat he was

43

suffering, but wouldn't admit it. I was not doing all that well myself, even with my being used to the hot weather in Florida. I finally spotted an escape from the work for a while. Nearby was the chapel, a Quonset hut building. I suggested to my companion we go inside and rest. We went in and low and behold it was air-conditioned. We were enjoying it mightily when a chaplain's aide came in to the building. He inquired to our purpose in the building and we told him we were just cooling off. After explaining the ditch digging we had been doing, he was kind enough to not run us out. Instead he had us put out some programs on the pews for the next service to keep us busy.

Another job we were assigned, and I can't remember how we 'volunteered' for it, was to go with a small convoy to a supply dump to pick up supplies. There was a first class in charge who pretty much kept to himself. When we arrived at the place we loaded the supplies which were the reason we were brought along in the first place. Sometime during the loading the crusty old salty First Class stripped off his shirt and I noticed he had a tattoo across his abdomen that said "Danger, Swinging Boom", he was for sure an old salt.

On the way back though he displayed a kinder side of himself when he broke open a case of half pint chocolate milk cartons and told us to help ourselves. We were passing through what was obviously not an affluent section of Vietnam. The roads were dirt and the buildings shabby. Children, toddlers mostly, were playing naked in front of the dirt entryways of homes with adults standing watching them and watching us go by. Apparently something they were used to. The First Class looking out as we passed by suddenly started tossing the remainder of the milk off the side of the truck to the small kids. Naked, and running alongside the truck while their parents shouted and laughed they scrambled for the milk. I looked at the First Class to see if he was smiling, but he wasn't, his face was impassive. I have often wondered what he was thinking as he watched those little kids pick up a milk carton and run back to their parents.

After passing through the village we crossed a river on the way to the supply dump and as we crossed, I noticed some square structures built along the sides of the bridge about twenty feet apart and about the size of a 3x3 cube and perhaps 3 feet high. I didn't know what they were for but soon found out. As we went by one of the structures a conical hat, the type that was commonly worn by the local Vietnamese, popped up over the top of the structure and a Vietnamese man casually watched us pass by. I suddenly realized the structure was a toilet that dumped in to the river and the man was doing his business.

Another job assigned to us was a trip down to the piers where a huge troop ship was coming in. We were sent down as line handlers if I remember correctly. I do remember the ship was ugly, and I didn't think I would care to cross an ocean in it. We saw a few soldiers on board but not many were out on deck for some reason or another.

My traveling companion and I went to the local base club (American one) where you could buy warm beer for 10 cents a can. The club had an outside deck or porch that you could sit out on. The day we did this we were entertained with some live fire going out to a hill across the bay from us and it was the first I had seen. There were several rounds fired at a hill which didn't seem that far from the base, and these may have been practice rounds, but I seem to remember the guy behind the bar saying there were Cong up there.

Perimeter emplacements Vung Tao Navy Base

That there were Viet Cong or NVN around was evidenced by the placement of sandbagged gun positions around the perimeter of the base

A Swift Boat Ride

Navy Swift boats patrolled the coastal areas of Vietnam to deter infiltration of men and weapons by the North Vietnamese.

Well, our vacation at Vung Tao was soon over and the good folks there loaded me and my companions in travel aboard a Navy Swift Boat, so we could continue to our destination. We were now headed down the Vietnamese coast, on the South China Sea, in a Swift boat, at night, during a war, oh joy; they didn't even issue us a weapon.

We left Vung Tao just before dark and headed out in to the South China Sea and by nightfall I couldn't see land and I didn't know if we were out that far or the coast just blended with the dark water. The boat had no inside or below deck accommodations, so we had to sleep on the deck with our baggage as a pillow. I don't remember much about the night other than it was a fitful sleep, and I was tired when I woke up.

During the night the Swift boat made is way down the coast from the Vung Tao Navy base and apparently their navigation was excellent or else their radar was as we hit the Delta dead on the next morning despite the darkness. I don't remember much of the trip other than being miserable on the hard deck, trying to sleep. I also don't remember eating anything that night but the next morning, before daylight, they let us go in to the tiny galley on the swift boat and fed us breakfast, eggs and bacon, so that was a big help in getting us going for the rest of the trip

As daylight approached, I noticed some objects starting to take shape in the dimness, almost like apparitions, and as we were moving along slowly I had time to study these as we passed but could not make out quite what they were until it became light enough to reveal that they were little houses, or hutches (pronounced hootches), built on tall stilts in the water. We had entered the mouth of the Bassac and as we passed in towards the river these buildings appeared out the mist and there were many of them. I did not see any people but as we passed by one a bucket suddenly dropped down from the bottom of one of the buildings and splashed in to the water where it rested a minute then went reeling back up. I'm not sure but I think it was probably a night bucket, or as the old country folks in the US used to call them, a slop jar. The night's deposits were probably being washed away in the river water but that is just a guess, could have been getting water for their morning tea, who knows.

The water at the mouth was starting to become a milky brown color, not brown like muddy brown but more of a coffee with cream brown. This was the color of water I would stare at for the better part of the next year.

After entering the mouth of the Bassac I'm not sure how far the Swift boat ran up before rendezvousing with a PBR from the Jennings County. We were transferred to the PBR which made the Swift boat seem like a luxury liner in size. The boat was small and was a design that had been created for the recreational market. They were converted to patrol boats for the river systems because of the propulsion they utilized which was a water jet type system with no propeller. This allowed for very shallow water operations.

After settling in on the PBR the crew started up the river. After a while they slowed down and gave us a demonstration of some weaponry on board one of which I remember is the grenade launcher, which they fired a round in to the jungle. It was a smaller version of a mortar that fired a grenade. There was also a machine gun on the bow and all the crew were armed with M-16 rifles.

As we rode up the river I noticed the palm trees on the bank were so thick it was like a jungle scene, I guess this plus the many canals along the banks were a haven for North Vietnamese and Viet Cong to operate in, using the rivers and canals to transport weapons and supplies.

Mekong Delta

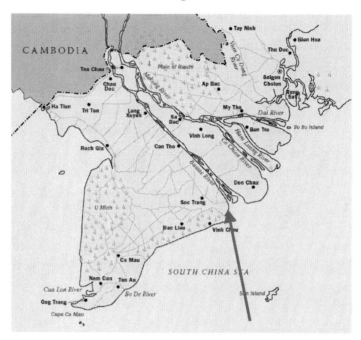

Area of operations for the USS Jennings County and her attached river squadrons of PBR's and Seawolf Helicopters. Bassac and Co Chien rivers. Large arrow is approximate area of PBR ride to meet the ship small arrow is location of Vung Tao

Photo from Collection, Archives Branch, Naval History and Heritage Command, Washington, DC

USS Jennings County LST-846
Mekong Delta

1967-1968

We were underway for an hour or two or maybe longer before the Jennings County hove in to view. She was no beauty for sure but to a guy who was impressed with anything larger than a Florida mullet boat it was a nice size vessel whose original purpose was to transport tanks and other equipment to landing areas on islands in the Pacific to support ground forces. The shallow draft of these LST ships made them ideal for the rivers in Vietnam having a draft of around 8 feet.

There were booms swung out from the sides, two to a side, with PBR's tied off here and there on the booms. As we came up to the side, I saw that our means of boarding was to be a small steel ladder attached to the side, not my idea of a safe method but I had no choice. The climb seemed to be a long one from way down on that PBR, but I managed to get on deck.

The topside deck of the ship was, to say the least, cluttered. There were two Seawolf helicopters on the tank deck area and various pieces of equipment and booms for lifting the boats out of the water to drop down in to the well deck for repairs. The well deck was used for tanks and other equipment during WWII during amphibious landings where the LST's would run up to the beach, open the well deck doors and the tanks would roll out on to the beach with the marines. For the Vietnam War the Jennings County had been modified to support the Riverine Forces in the Mekong Delta. The well deck was converted in to a floating repair shop for the PBR's and the main deck became a helo pad for the Seawolf helicopters.

There was no room to spare on the crowded and busy main deck of the Jennings County. The narrow gap between the helo and the safety net on the side (where the crewman is walking) was all the room the landing signalman had when guiding the choppers in. This photo shows a PBR being lowered in to the well deck for maintenance or repairs. I rode one of the Huey helicopters off the ship when I was selected to attend the Bob Hope show, which due to some paperwork problems I never made it to. Photo: Online source

My companions and I were escorted down to the ships office and checked in. I was assigned to a berthing compartment but at the time not with the Operations department crew and I luckily wound up with a bottom rack, unfortunately it was right next to a hatch that was very busy with the comings and goings of the crew. The compartments had been retrofitted with air conditioning and sometimes failed, usually when I was trying to sleep while off watch. The entry in to the berthing areas was through a door outside the end of the galley passageway, one on the Port and one on the Starboard sides. It was a shotgun arrangement, and you had to pass through any compartments to get to yours depending on which one it was. Mine was the third compartment, so I passed through two before entering it. My compartments other end was abutted against the head. The racks, or beds, were arranged on each side of the compartments which are narrow to begin with and with bunks on each side and lockers by the bunks it made the passageway narrow and these passageways could be busy at times as it was the only route to the head and to various other comparts, engineering access hatches and storerooms. My initial assigned rack was in an area of supply personnel the two directly across was a Pilipino wardroom steward and the other a galley cook. I was eventually assigned another rack in the compartment on the forward side of the head which held all operations personnel.

There are a couple of memorable things I remember about sleeping in these compartments. One was the time we had a Seal team on board and one Seal was assigned to an empty bunk above me, I came down to go to bed and he was laying in his bunk, naked with a shotgun laying by his side. I did not question that method of repose and slept a bit uneasy that night being a little afraid that if I moved around too much, he would be startled awake and use that shotgun on me. They were not around long, and he soon was gone.

Another time I was assigned a temporary bunk which was directly over a hatch of a storeroom and when the cooks needed stores, they would lift my bunk up and trice it (latch in in the upright position). This was ok during the time when I was on watch and not in it but when I was sleeping, it didn't bother them a bit to lift the bunk up and trice it with me in it and they were not quite about it either.

All in all, the tiny rack and a small locker with all my possessions would soon became a little home area to me. There were no coffin lockers with the plentiful storage space I would have on future ship assignments nor were there any privacy curtains or a bunk light. With the port and starboard watch rotations and the sleep deprivation you experience with this type shift work the thin mattress and noisy surroundings soon cease to bother you. I was once told you finally know when you're a true sailor when you can fall asleep anywhere at any time under any conditions, even standing up. I'm not sure I ever quite reached that point of sleeping standing up, but I came close a few times.

The berthing compartment, the mess deck and the Radio Shack became the three areas my daily routine would revolve around, as it did for much of the crew.

Jennings County Radio Shack

After checking in and being assigned a bunk I was next taken to the Radio Shack but was informed that until my security clearance was finalized, I would be working in the CIC (Combat Information Center). I was assigned in that area to stand watch on the depth sounder scope. This was a big round scope with a rubber skirt over the screen and a viewing port in the top of the rubber that fit the eyes allowing light to be blocked. I found out that the contour of bottom of the bottom tended to fluctuate rapidly when we were moving on the river making it hard to provide a sensible sounding to the bridge watch and it was hairy for a while until I got the hang of it. Today I have a $99.00 fish finder in my boat that tells me more than that monster did, I can see fish, get the depth and temperature of the water at a glance in the sun, no hood required.

I quickly settled in and soon was standing watches in the Radio Shack. It became a routine of stand watch, eat chow, do field day in berthing and the head if you were coming off the mid watch otherwise you usually went to bed. Coming off the day watch you could stay up for movie call on the mess deck if you were willing to lose the 2 hours of precious sleep it cost you.

The galley on the ship was at the aft end of the ship on the main deck. The line for chow went in a hatch on the starboard side and passed down the serving line at the end which you would carry your tray down a ladder to the deck down one level where the tables were located. If you didn't go down that hatch you would exit through a hatch on the port side to the open deck. Just before the port exit there was a door to the right that entered Officers country. The standard drink for chow was the famous Navy bug juice (A high powered form of Kool Aid, loaded with sugar) There was also a milk dispenser, rarely used for real milk, and a coffee machine. The food was not bad considering what the cooks had to work with. Resupply was by a barge that came up the river at infrequent intervals. I'm not sure but I Believe Vung Tao was also the supply support for the Riverine forces, so this resupply may have been from that location but I'm not positive.

Life aboard the Jennings County quickly settled in to a routine of port and starboard watches that is 8 hours on and 8 hours off seven days a week although the eight hours off generally involved cleaning the berthing compartments and heads (bathrooms) for the off mid watch before going to bed.

The ship was a busy unit and there seemed to be something going on all the time. The PBR's came and went on patrol as did the Seawolf helicopters. The deck crew still did routine cleaning and maintenance topside and the other departments were busy doing their jobs whether it be in the engine room, the galley, the ships laundry or ships office. It was a fully functional US Navy ship in every way just in a different setting, up a river in the Mekong Delta in a war zone. You could get a haircut from the ships barber or buy a pack of cigarettes from the ships store. You could laze around and take it easy on a day off but there were few of those, actually I don't think there were any.

I quickly learned the ropes of watch-standing and all the various duties of a shipboard Radioman, you couldn't help but learn the ropes quickly as that was pretty much all you did seven days a week. Our primary function was to process incoming and outgoing radio Teletype messages. The incoming part consisted of taking messages that had come in over the Fleet Broadcast circuit and preparing them to distribution to the various officers and departments on board. The method on this ship, which was limited in accessories for processing such as a duplicating machine, was to retype the single copy of the Teletype message on to a carbon form which had seven copies. These had to be retyped word for word and it was boring but easy. The outgoing processing consisted of taking rough drafts brought to radio and punching them up on the Teletype machine on Teletype tape. We would then take it to the person for proof reading and any changes prior to sending the final copy to whatever station we could contact at the time of day we were transmitting which depended on the radio band conditions. Band condition changed with the atmospheric layers as they shifted around during the day or night. Usually the Naval Communications Station at Camh Rhan Bay was our main go to station, but sometimes we had to resort to sending to other stations if we could such as Navcams Pearl Harbor or the NAVCOMSTA in the Panama Canal.

Other radio operations that were going in the shack were the tactical radios that were used to communicate with the PBR's and Seawolf helicopters during operations or patrols. These were in radio in a cubbyhole area and pretty much once set they did not need any tending to, but we could listen in on any action going on and occasionally it was interesting. The shack consisted of this area the main area and a secure Teletype area and all three together would be about the size of a modern-day house bathroom.

Communications between the various support platforms, other than tactical radio, was a Teletype link simply called an Orestes circuit. This was what was known as a simplex (one way at a time) that we used to exchange message traffic between our ship and the other TF 116 units on the rivers which included USS Hunterdon County, USS Garrett County and the USS Garnett County. There was also an Army barge that was on the circuit.

As I have already said the routine soon became, well routine. I was quickly bored with the constant watch standing and had little to do on mid watches other than the excitement of the chatter on the tactical radios during a fire fight. These radios were operated by the Combat Information Center watch

58

standers and are only job was to make sure the radios were on the correct frequency and working. Mostly we looked forward to getting off watch and eating since there was nothing much else to break up the monotony.

My memory from 50 years down the road has prevented me from remembering many of the names of the people I served with on the Jennings County. I do remember RM1 McCloud; I believe he was from North Dakota; he was a good LPO and dealt fairly with the whole gang. There was an RMSN I went through A school with whose name I can't recall but he was from New York and had worked in banks prior to joining the Navy. There was an RMSN who called himself FUBAR (Fouled Up Beyond all Recognition) and was the person who got me involved in taking photographs. I bought a 35mm camera and started taking B&W photographs and later slides. I still have some slides but have not seen any of the B&W photographs in years and are either lost or I threw them out. There was an RMSN who was the RM gang gambler, he would play craps down in the well deck area in some hidden location. I don't recall his name either but may have been Huffman. There were others in the radio gang that I just can't remember the names of, but all were excellent Radioman and I don't recall any disciplinary problems in the gang and that was most likely because we had such a strong leader with RM1 McCloud who first got my attention over an incident with making coffee.

I didn't drink coffee when I joined the Navy and after a year and a half still didn't drink it when I checked on board the Jennings County. The Navy tradition in those days was the junior guy made the coffee, and I was that guy in my section. I refused to make it because I didn't drink it, justification in my mind. The RM1 had a different idea on that however he didn't bust my chops. He got crafty. He used a scare tactic that changed my mind quickly as one day when I refused during the day watch when he was in the shack he said "ok, let's go see the

59

XO" It's one of those Oh Shit moments when you think you may have pushed back to hard. Well the XO was an academy graduate, a Lieutenant Keogh. He was calm as he explained about Navy tradition and said he had also had his share of being the bottom man and having to do things he didn't exactly relish. I was happy to get out of there with just a talking to and after that I made the coffee, and I also started drinking it and still do. Guess I was finally becoming a real sailor, despite myself.

I came too much admire LT Keogh, he was the type who not only tells you something was not correct but would tell you how to correct it. For example, one day when I was doing a field-day the head for our berthing area I had worked extremely hard to get an outstanding, but he hit me for water spots on the mirrors. I explained to him I had washed them all and the spots still showed. He asked me to go round up some newspaper, which I did, probably the Stars and Stripes since I don't know what else we would have had available. But I did find some, and he took the newspaper and while I watched he rubbed a mirror to a perfect shine with wadded up newspaper. I was impressed, and he said to me as he left that he had "I learned that trick at the Academy".

The radio shack itself was small and crowded with equipment. The main part, Radio Central, was longer than wide, ran aft to forward with an operator's desk facing the port bulkhead on which sat a typewriter for typing up the "flimsies" (already mentioned but which means transferring the information from the canary yellow Teletype copy that came in over the Navy Fleet Broadcast system in order to have multiple copies). As you entered the door to Radio, you were in the radio central part and to the left through a small hatch is where the Radio Teletype room was located where the messages came in through radio receivers and were transmitted out on various Teletype machines with the radio transmitters. This room also housed the encryption equipment. This area was even smaller and more crowded than central.

On the forward end of Radio Central and behind a rack of equipment was the tactical radio area, this was where the VHF radios were installed for the PBR units that communicated to the ship and to each other using these type radios. The Operations Specialists in the Combat Information Center manned the ships end of these radios. Most of the communications was in the clear but coordinates and positions were always encrypted and anytime this would be done the operator would say "shackle" read the encrypted part and then say "unshackle" indicated they were going back to clear mode.

Back on the radio central part on the other side of the rack of equipment there was one radio that intrigued me, mainly because it didn't work, after a while, during slack periods, I decided to play around with this radio and see if I could get it to work. Its nomenclature was AN/URC-32 and the only HF transceiver in the shack, a modular style radio it was quirky to tune. The other radios were either transceivers or receivers and were tuned separately, this one you tuned both at the same time. I spent many an hour tuning and re-tuning this radio but never got it to work. A radio tech also came by to work on it and couldn't get it to work either. The radio came to be a radio central ornament of no use apparently an advance in a technology that had not been tested under shipboard conditions.

The daily watch routine of sending, receiving and distributing message traffic was not difficult other than the nightly hassle to keep frequencies tuned up during the night hours and the only physically hard work was the nightly field day and that too wasn't bad as usually two were sharing the work.

AN\URC-32. The complexity of this radio seemed to possess me. Never did get it to work.

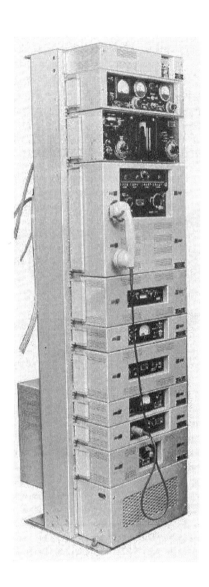

The URC-32 wasn't the only thing that the Radio Shack had that peaked my interest. We had a port call in Hong Kong on the return to Mekong from the refit we did at Subic Bay. Hong Kong at that time was a British Colony and one of the port entry requirements was to check in with the Harbor Control on a CW (Morse code) circuit. Now my CW had been pretty much idle since Radioman School, but I still knew it well and decided to practice in case I was on watch when we had to check in. The problem though, for me, was that sitting at the operator's position along with the straight key was also a device known in the Radio Shack as a "bug". This was a Vibro-plex semi-automatic CW (Continuous Wave meaning Morse Code) sender. It was a mechanical sender using springs and other items in a way that would automatically generate either dots or dashes when you operated the paddle. The paddle was positioned vertically, and the thumb would press the left side of the paddle to generate dots and the index finger would press the right side to produce dashes. It was fast too, fast. Well, the thing fascinated me to no end, much like the AN\URC-32. I started playing around with it and got to where I could send the letter V really fast. I then moved on to sending our call sign and could also send that out at a blazing speed.

By the time we were getting ready to enter the harbor I thought I could use the bug to check in and was on watch when we started picking up the traffic on the check-in net. I sent several calls as fast as I could work the bug and didn't receive any answer. I was having fun and since most of the CW I heard on the net was not all that fast I thought I was really the hot operator. Then on about my fifth attempt the Brits answered, and boy they blistered my ass good, it sounded like 50wpm and I had no clue what they were sending. I went to in to shock for a few seconds then being that I was alone at the time, my co-watch stander was in the other room, I did the only thing I could

63

think to do, I pretended I didn't hear it. I didn't make any more attempts leaving the check-in for the next watch. Lesson learned. I don't think I ever touched another Vibro-plex bug after that.

Vibro-plex Morse Code keyer known as the 'Bug' by Navy Radioman. I never mastered it.

Life around the Ship

I did other things other than stand watches and test the RM1's patience with coffee making, like one evening I was assigned to supervise a guy from engineering that had been given extra duty for some infraction and it was most likely from shooting his mouth off from what I figured after listening to him for just a few minutes. I had him start cleaning the head, and he complained and griped about anything and everything and I was worried he would give me a hard time and I was still only a seaman, but he did what I told him to do. Just before we finished the head he suddenly remembered he was supposed to fill a tank with lime on the ships evaporators. So, I escorted this guy, after he picked up a bag of lime, through the well deck and almost to the bow end of the well deck where he stopped, put the bag down and then opened a small hatch, picked up the bag of lime opened it and poured the entire bag down the opened hatch. I had no clue what he was doing, or even if he was supposed to be doing it, I had just taken his word he was supposed to do this, why else would you want to lug a heavy bag around. He actually explained to me about the evaporators and it was then realized that the water we were drinking on board the Jennings County was being made out of the brown silty waters of the Mekong River we were patrolling and I had seen water buffalo more than once standing belly deep along the edges and I knew from my growing up in a rural county what cows and bulls do more than anything other than eat, and that was to crap. I didn't worry much about it though as mostly I drank bug juice and no germ could live in that stuff.

Another interesting thing that happened was shortly after I arrived on board the Jennings County the Aircraft Carrier USS Forrestal had a flight deck accident involving some old unstable bombs that blasted a hole in the flight deck and caused great damage and killed over a hundred sailors. At the time it was interesting news and being a Radioman you get to see the message traffic coming through from and to the other ships in the area so we had firsthand news coming in on the accident and little did I know at the time that seven years later I would be assigned to the Forrestal and spend two years aboard her making two Mediterranean cruises while assigned one in 1975 and one in 1976.

The ship was small and though the berthing was cramped for everyone, Officers and crew, some senior ranks found a way to isolate themselves in a fashion. The senior Petty Officers, mainly the First-Class Petty Officers, would in the evenings after chow gather as a group on the bow area under the gun tubs. This was their way of being able to share sea stories and bounce problems off one another without the younger ranks close by to eavesdrop. I suspect this congregating of senior enlisted has been a Navy tradition since sailing ships roamed the oceans and of course the younger sailors would, out of hearing of these senior Petty Officers of course, make fun of it as most looked at any sailor who enlisted for more than one term as a lifer. On the Jennings County this area became known as "Lifers Roost" and it was an unofficial off-limits area for any but the senior ranks during these get to gather and none of the lowly enlisted dared violate it.

As the days stretched out, and I was able to observe more of the daily operations of the Jennings County, I came to realize that there was a lot going on. I liked to go on deck prior to an eve watch and just check out what Patrol boats were tied out on the booms or if the Seawolf choppers were on deck. I watched one day as the first-class Boatswain mate used the crane to winch a PBR into the Well Deck and then another day was standing on deck when a Seal detachment came on board and had with them a German Shepard dog. There was the time that a rocket launcher was set up in the open hatch of the Well Deck and test fired. It was one of those that I had seen on black and white footage on TV from WWII. There was also the day that a captured Viet Cong was brought aboard, they had him on the 02 deck and he was surrounded by several RVN officers. Not sure what ever happened to him as I didn't get to hang around long, had to go on watch. There was just a lot that went on after all it was a war zone. One day a sampan pulled up that had a sick person on it and the Corpsman (Doc) went down the vertical ladder on the side and checked it out. Again, I didn't get to hang around but to a 20-year-old this was all interesting stuff.

The detachments of PBRs and Seawolfs were always doing something, either leaving on patrols or some other operation or maintaining their boats or aircraft. These were the people who put their lives on the line on every patrol.

These detachments were the reason for the Jennings County being in the river, to provide support for the crews and equipment that were constantly roaming the river on patrol. The river itself, which in the first part of my tour was the Bassac River, was a coffee with cream color, not exactly muddy but not the black tannic colors I was used to from the Rivers in Florida. The width varied but was a wide river and the Jennings County didn't seem to have much trouble navigating or maneuvering in it. Along the banks, on any given day, we might pass villages

67

were farmers could be seen working in the paddies or spot a water buffalo standing up to its hocks on the river edge. The sunsets on the river impressed me with their colors and I took some photographs of several which have long since been lost. The weather was tropical warm and not unpleasant, at least on the river it was not that pleasant, I imagine back in the jungles or canals along the river. Today you can book a cruise on the rivers and enjoy them with all the amenities of a tourist please cruise. But back to the reality of the Jennings County it was anything but a cruise boat.

Since I had no previous ship assignments for comparison, my impression of the USS Jennings County was one of acceptance and I don't remember knocking the ship or do I remember others on board doing so. She was a ship I was on and that was about as far as I thought it out. I knew she was not the picture of a Naval Warship that in most people's minds when they think of a warship, sleek and mean looking with big gun mounts like the ships that tied up at the pier in Key West that I sometimes line handled for, but later on, many years later, I would come to understand that she was one of the unsung heroes of the Navy and on that note I will insert a piece here regarding the career of this veteran of three wars.

An Unsung Hero

USS Jennings County LST-846

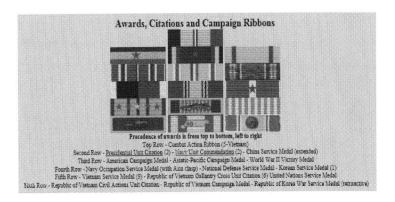

Awards, Citations and Campaign Ribbons

Precedence of awards is from top to bottom, left to right
Top Row - Combat Action Ribbon (5-Vietnam)
Second Row - Presidential Unit Citation (2) - Navy Unit Commendation (2) - China Service Medal (extended)
Third Row - American Campaign Medal - Asiatic-Pacific Campaign Medal - World War II Victory Medal
Fourth Row - Navy Occupation Service Medal (with Asia clasp) - National Defense Service Medal - Korean Service Medal (1)
Fifth Row - Vietnam Service Medal (9) - Republic of Vietnam Gallantry Cross Unit Citation (6) United Nations Service Medal
Sixth Row - Republic of Vietnam Civil Actions Unit Citation - Republic of Vietnam Campaign Medal - Republic of Korea War Service Medal (retroactive)

When I came aboard the USS Jennings County, LST-846, in July 1967 she was patrolling the Bassac River and later shifted over to the Co Chien River (I think around the last half of my time aboard). She patrolled, pulling her boom attached PBR's along with her if there were any tied off to them, up and down wherever the current situation or assignments took her. Assigned to the ship were somewhere around 10 PBR (Patrol Boat, River) and 2 Sea wolf Helicopters with an occasional stay by a Navy Seal team. Ships Company was mainly support personnel for these detachments and for operating the ship as the mother base for the units. I was part of the Radio Gang and if I remember correctly consisted of around 8 Radioman of various ranks. The ship's crew also manned the weapons onboard which consisted of fore-and-aft gun tubs with 40mm antiaircraft guns mounted. These were used for gunfire support. Also, there were machine guns mounted at several locations. Depending on what our position in the river was if we were close enough to the banks they could also double as gunfire support.

The ship, having a flat front and no keel since it was designed to run up on the beach and land equipment, rode very rough with lots of rolling. The joke during WWII was that they would even roll in dry dock.

Launched in December 1944 the history of the ship goes back to World War II when she supported operations in Guam, the Marshall Islands and Okinawa.

After WWII she remained in the Pacific providing cargo support for occupation troops also during this period, she made a trip to Indo China. She was decommissioned in 1949.

After the outbreak of the Korean conflict she was recommissioned in November 1950 and supported operations in the area until 1954. Her first participation in Indo China was in support of French troops transporting troops and vehicles along the coast of Indochina. She also performed duties during Operation Passage to Freedom transporting Vietnamese from North to South Vietnam after the partitioning of the country. She returned to the States in 1955 and was decommissioned at San Diego in December 1955.

After ten years with the Pacific Reserve Fleet she was recommissioned on 11 June 1966 to support U.S. forces in South Vietnam. Jennings County departed San Diego on 11 September, arriving at Chu Lai on 11 November. For the remainder of 1966 she conducted river patrols and in 1967 she continued her patrols supporting "Game Warden" operations. In 1970, while off the coast of Son on Doc at the southern tip of Viet Nam she suffered a serious fire in her galley that rendered her unable to continue supporting her on-board crew. She was removed from station, and later, the USS Garrett County, LST-786 took her place as a river boat tender in support of river control operations.

The USS Jennings County had many decorations for her wartime service across three separate wars. She was also one of the American warships present in Tokyo Bay during the surrender ceremonies when Japan surrendered to Douglas MacArthur on board the USS Missouri.

Jennings County the year before decommissioning in 1949

The Vietnam war in 1967 was not the Jennings County's first tour in Indo China, this photo is somewhere between 1946 and 1949.

Recommissioning for Vietnam ceremony

Jennings County is recommissioned in 1966 to active duty and will become the first of the mother ships for the Riverine Force Vietnam.

Jennings County river operations

View of the USS Jennings County from the Port Bow. This was much the way it was when I was on board. A Seawolf is landing from the Starboard side and was the reason I included the photograph even though it's of poor quality. There are several PBR's tied off to booms and there is a partial view of one of the 40mm gun tubs on the Port Side Bow.

On the O1 level, behind the crane boom was the entry hatch to Radio Central where a second regular door entry that had a window for passing traffic through was located. There was also a ladder leading down from the entry into Officers Country and one of my first jobs was carrying a covered clip board around to all the officers' staterooms, so they could review the nights incoming message traffic and take copies they needed.

Fore and Aft views of the Jennings County

Bow and Stern shots with Seawolfs and showing gun tubs

During the Vietnam War USS Jennings County (LST-846) participated in the following campaigns:

▮▮▮▮▮ Vietnam War Campaigns	
Campaign and Dates	**Campaign and Dates**
Vietnamese Counteroffensive - Phase II 7 November to 31 December 1966 11 March to 31 May 1967	**Vietnam Summer-Fall 1969** 9 June to 14 September 1969 14 to 31 October 1969
Vietnamese Counteroffensive - Phase III 1 June to 26 August 1967 12 October 1967 to 29 January 1968	**Vietnam Winter-Spring 1969** 1 November 1969 to 1 April 1970
Tet Counteroffensive 30 January to 1 April 1968	**Sanctuary Counteroffensive** 1 to 30 June 1970
Vietnamese Counteroffensive - Phase IV 2 to 14 April 1968 26 April to 9 June 1968	**Vietnamese Counteroffensive - Phase VII** 30 June to 12 August 1970
Tet 69/Counteroffensive 1 May to 8 June 1969	

From Navsource.org

75

A visit to a Vietnamese river village

And a busted trip to the Bob Hope Show

As I have already alluded to the shipboard routine had become, well, routine and boring for the most part. One day though we the ship anchored across from a small village on the river bank and we got a break from the routine. We were told that we would be allowed to go over for some recreation, meaning drinking warm beer, at the village and to consider it a goodwill visit and be nice to the natives. I went over with a QM1 (Quartermaster) on the ships LCVP (Landing Craft Vehicle and Personnel). The QM1 had been my supervisor when I was assigned to CIC when waiting on my clearance for Radio. We walked around the village and stared at the Vietnamese and they stared at us. Of course, it only took a couple of the warm Slitz beers to light us up and the QM1 was really lit. We went over to where a Vietnamese sailor was manning a machine gun in a sand-bagged emplacement and was trying to carry on a conversation with him which mostly meant hand gestures. The QM1 wanted to trade his US Navy Dungaree shirt with the Vietnamese sailor's uniform cotton shirt; I remember it was a light purple color. It started raining during the negotiations and when I say rain I mean a pouring down monsoon like rain. No matter to the QM1 he continued to try to trade shirts and finally the Vietnamese sailor understood what he wanted to do and readily did the swap since he was getting the better shirt. We left to board the LCVP to return to the ship with the QM1 looking a bit ludicrous in the tight-fitting Vietnamese Navy shirt, but he had his souvenir and was happy, and drunk.

I don't remember the exact dates maybe December 1967 I was selected to represent the Operations department on the ship as an attendee at the Bob Hope show in Saigon. I was ok with that as it would get me off the ship for a few days. There were four of us if I remember correctly. I was the lowest ranking and youngest I think with the oldest being an Engineman First Class (EM1) who was the ranking Petty Officer of our little group. All were in dungarees except me, I opted to wear the greens we were authorized to wear while assigned to the Jennings County since I thought they would be better to travel in, I only had one set, so I took a set of dungarees with me.

We were ferried to Binh Thuy by our onboard Seawolf helicopters. I was on the one with one other selectee and sat in the middle position between him and the door gunner who was wearing a helmet with goggles and sort of hung at the outer edge of the open door with his hands always on the gun. I thought hanging out a door in flight was too scary to be something I would volunteer for he seemed at home with the position. He was a nice guy and later we would hang out a little after duty hours and sometimes eat chow together depending on each of our schedules. The chopper took off up the river and boy it was some kind of ride. I had never been on one before and was totally absorbed in the mechanics of the ship, watching the pilot work the controls. After a little while running up the river the pilot went inland towards a building which I was gold be the door gunner was a known Viet Cong stopping place, an old church, and the pilot fired off two of the rockets from the side pods mounted on the chopper at the building. This was exciting, but I was glad no one fired back. We then went on and landed at Binh Thuy.

Our little group caught a shuttle bus that went to the Air Base at Can Tho, I believe it was Can Tho, maybe not, where we were to catch a hop by military aircraft to Saigon. We got to the airbase and the First Class presented our paperwork and we all were high with an excitement which was dashed almost immediately by the person processing the flights who said the paperwork was not correct and he could not board us to fly to Saigon. Nothing would persuade the person to make an exception and there was no way to reach out to the ship for help. We all dejectedly headed over to the base cafeteria to get something to eat. We also bought some beer and started drinking. After a while we met a couple of other guys drinking beer who were in the army who joined us drinking beer. Soon we became friends and when we decided to leave they offered us a place to sleep at their post. The other guys with me opted to go in to town but I was pretty done in with the travel and drinking and went to the post with the two Army guys and crashed in a bunk that was in a huge Army green tent being used for barracks. It was okay until morning when a shouting Army Sargent came in to the tent and started yelling for everyone to fall out walking around and kicking bunks, including the one I was in. I was thinking I as up shit creek and was about to be sent in to the Jungle on an Army patrol but fortunately the two guys who had offered me the place to sleep intervened and said I was a guest for the night and was Navy; the Sargent looked at me and said to the two men to get me out of his tent. The two guys I had befriended said not to worry that they were cooks, and the sergeants didn't screw with them, but I hurriedly left anyway.

I caught a ride in an army truck at the front gate of the post and when I climbed in with a couple of other grunts in to the back (picture WWII troop transport truck) I took a seat on the bench on the right side. Both sides had soldiers, and I was the only sailor, but I was wearing Navy greens, so I didn't stand out too bad. The interior was a bit dim since it was early in the morning but as the light improved, I could see more detail and the soldier next to me appeared to be wearing some sort of rolled up scarf or other piece of clothing around his neck. I didn't think it was cool enough for that but wasn't about to say anything about it. After a while the soldier who apparently was trying to nap, stirred, reached up and unwrapped the scarf and the scarf started to move! I realized then it was a snake, a small anaconda type if my guess was right. I sat very still until we reached the gate at Bien Thuy and I was more than happy to bail out of that ride!

I entered the gate at Bien Thuy and asked the guard where the communications shack was; he directed me to the building it was in and I range the entry bell and asked for the operator I knew from working the Teletype circuits we used to maintain communications between the various river patrol units. He happened to be coming off the mid watch and was very helpful in allowing me use of his end of the circuit to contact the Jennings County and let them know we had not been able to fly out to Saigon and that I was at the Bien Thuy base and needed transport to the ship.

The Radioman operator that helped me took me to the chow hall where we ate and then I sat and waited all day for the PBR to arrive that would take me back to the ship. A PBR finally showed up and guess who was aboard? The Skipper himself and he had one fierce look on his face when I stepped on the PBR. He ordered me to sit on the back end of the boat, the wet spot, and that is where I rode on the return to the ship.

I got aboard late, around 10 or 11 PM and I went to bed tired and glad it was over. About 30 minutes later a First Class (not the one in charge) woke me and told me I had the mid watch, I was incredulous! I said I just got back and was tired, but he would have none of it. So, I drug myself up to the Radio Shack and stood the mid watch. What an inglorious comedown from two days prior when I was sky high with excitement from being selected to go to the Bob Hope show as a representative for my department. I felt bad but also knew it was nothing I could have done anything about since it was a paperwork foul up, and to be honest no one was faulting me as far as I knew. The rest of the group finally showed up and I don't know how their return went over.

Well, the routine was still, well routine, and I was back to port and starboard rotating watches, boring but sometimes interesting, especially when the PBR's or Seawolf helicopters got in to a fire fight and the tactical radios lit up with a fast and furious exchange of transmissions. Little did I know that not too long after my aborted trip to the Bob Hope Show we would be involved in what would become one of the most important battles of the Vietnam War, the Vietnamese New Year's Holiday Tet offensive.

Tet Offensive
January 1968

The Tet Offensive: A Turning Point

· In January of 1968, the Vietcong launched surprise attacks on cities throughout South Vietnam.

· The American embassy was attacked as well in the South Vietnamese capital of Saigon.

Even though the LST's like the USS Jennings County seemed to be a safe place to be during any combat situation, considering they were made of steel, they were slow moving flat bottom boats which made them ideal for the mother ship role they played for the PBR force but also placed them at risk in the narrow river systems that they had to operate in. On September 12, 1968, USS HUNTERDON COUNTY, another unsung hero of three wars, was ambushed near Ben Tre. I was not a witness to this attack, as my ship and the Hunterdon were on two different rivers in the Delta. When the attack started I was on watch and the operator on the Hunterdon begin sending flash reports on the Task Force Teletype circuit and I was able first hand see these reports. I don't remember the details of the

81

message but I later researched the attach and she was hit by rocket and recoilless rifle fire from shore suffering extensive structural damage. Two crewmen were killed and another twenty-five were wounded.

The constant danger of a swimmer attacks dictated the constant dropping of concussion grenades along the sides of the Jennings County at periodic intervals to deter the swimmers from attaching explosives on the hulls. These were not small concussions by any means, and if you happened to have a rack (bunk) near the hull (and these ships were thin hulled) the concussion could be jarring and would definitely upset your sleep for a while. You got used to them and knew why they were being used, but it was still a hated but a necessary thing. From what I remember the constant battering from these grenades eventually split a seam on the Jennings County requiring a yard period in Yokosuka, Japan for repairs. This may not be totally factual, but seems to be what I recall. This would be near the end of my tour and I would transfer from the ship in Yokosuka.

On Jan 30, 1968 the Viet Cong and the North Vietnam Army undertook a massive infiltration of South Vietnam and launched multiple attacks throughout the country. The big news would be the fighting around Hue and Saigon but there were many other battles going on, including in the Delta.

At some point the ship anchored off the bank near the Navy detachment at Bien Thuy and started providing fire support for the base. I went up to the Radio Shack early and as I opened the hatch to the outside deck from the starboard side galley entryway I needed go left to traverse to the ladder that ascended to the Radio Shack. As I exited out, and it was dark, so I slid to the side and closed the hatch to let my eyes adjust but about that time a 7.62 mm machine gun set up at that spot starting firing, at what I don't know, but I spent a few seconds admiring the tracers when I figured I better move on. A little further down where the ladder was I decided to go on past and peek around the corner of the bulkhead to observe the gun tubs in action, and they were pumping a lot of shells out at about that time.

The light from the guns illuminated in brief flashes an eerie scene of a cook, with his white Chefs hat still on his head, bobbing up and down to pass 40mm ammo clips to the loader. That was something I have never forgotten. I think this was the same cook who would bring pastry up to Radio during the mid-watch and in exchange we would put on music tapes he liked on the ships entertainment system.

The 1968 TET cease fire had fallen apart and the NVN and Viet Cong had managed to infiltrate and stage thousands of troops at many locations. They were invading Saigon and places such as Hue where the marines would have a rough go before pushing them out. I don't remember all the details, but the Jennings County had moved up to provide gun fire support to units close in to the river. We fired quite a lot that night from our 40mm gun tubs and I don't know the results. We would not really understand the depth and scope of the offensive until later as would a lot of other US Military folks.

The Navy River Patrol force had not been adequate to catch all the infiltrating troops or the weapons they were running up the river systems which would lead to the complete reforming and changing of tactics after the offensive. The North Vietnamese Navy, as it was discovered later, was so predictable in their patrol checks that the NVN and Cong had no trouble evading them. The operational name the Navy had for patrolling the rivers was Operation Game Warden. After 1968 it would go on to be one of the most successful operations during the Vietnam conflict and the US forces would have knocked the communists back and the war could have been over if it had been prosecuted correctly.

The North Vietnamese had also found a new weapon in the burgeoning antiwar protests that were heating up in the US. Eventually we would find a way to leave Vietnam, honorably as Richard Nixon put it, but we would not shake the curse for many years. I didn't feel like the military was again the respected organization it had been just after WWII until the Gulf war in 1990.

A War Death

After Tet the ships routine again returned to, well, routine. I began to look forward to completing my year on board and we found out later that due to the constant setting off of concussion grenades around the ship (too thwart sappers from setting charges, something that had happened to other units on the river) we had developed a crack in the front of the well deck and would have to go to the yards in Yokosuka, Japan. One other incident happened before I departed Vietnam.

I was on watch when the window bell rang alerting me that someone was at the window with message traffic. I opened it and recognized the pilot of the helicopter I had flown aboard on the aborted trip to the Bob Hope show (that we didn't make it to). He handed me CASEREP form (Casualty Report) for transmission and seemed to give me a direct look before leaving. I soon realized why he had the look, I read through the report and the name on it was my helicopter gunner friend.

The summary of the action as I remember it reported he had taken a round that entered underneath his helmet edge and died from the wound. It was hard to believe, but I had to send the message. I was alone at the time, so I punched the paper tape message and transmitted it. I must have forced something to deaden my feelings about the incident, and I don't know why, but I soon, over the years, forgot his name and never thought much about him until one day on the internet a niece of his posted a photo of him standing beside the helicopter on the deck of the USS Jennings County. She was asking if anyone knew the ships name. I responded but heard nothing back from her. The posting I responded to was several years old when I ran across it so most likely she never got the response. She had his name in the email and it was Chris. Later I read a posting that he had survived but eventually died from the wound in 1975.

But I, distinctly, remember the message had said he was found dead at his machine gun position on landing.

Boy, what a pose, me outside the hatch to Radio Central

USS Jennings County 1967-68

We sail to Yokosuka and I go back to the USA

We departed the Mekong Delta River system sometime in June 1968. We entered the yards in Yokosuka for repairs and shipboard routine became dry dock routine. As far as the Radio Gang was concerned it was one duty day in three in radio and the other two would be spent either painting or cleaning. The division I belonged to was moved from our regular compartment, so it could be refurbished and relocated to the aft compartments that had no air conditioning and it was miserable. I was almost happy to stand radio watches since it did have AC. I also tacked on my third-class crow (Petty Officer Third Class) while there. Times were good while in Yokosuka and the daily work was not hard, but I was looking forward to getting back to the USA and home. It was a year since I had seen family other than a two-day meeting with my older brother Wayne who was in port Subic Bay, Philippines during one of our three-day refits.

I could make a choice of a homeport location since I had served a year in-country in Vietnam. I, of course, chose Mayport, Florida and was assigned to the USS Stribling, DD-867, another WWII era ship commissioned in 1945 late but did not see action in that war.

I left the USS Jennings County, still in dry dock, sometime near the end of July 1968. The small ship was barely visible above the walls of the dry dock and she still was not the dashing war fighting ship most people picture as being part the Navy's powerhouse fleet, but she had done her job while I was on board and would be returning to Vietnam to resume patrol operations as she had been doing when we left. She would not be much longer a part of the River Patrol Force as she suffered a galley fire in late 1969 that rendered here unusable for the operation. The last I could find out about this unsung hero of a ship was a posting on the internet of a photo reportedly showing here anchored in Danang Harbor, South Vietnam. The belief I have is she was turned over to the South Vietnamese Navy and eventually sold, scrapped or converted to other use by the victorious North Vietnamese when they eventually took control of the entire country of Vietnam. That is just a guess though and if true was an ignoble end to a ship that had served well and earned many decorations and awards over a career that including participating in three wars. But I was moving on to another chapter of my Navy career and little did I know as I caught a taxi to the Tokyo airport that I was not yet done with South Vietnam.

I flew from Tokyo in August 1968 and after spending leave at home reported to Mayport for my next ship.

The only memorable incident on my return trip to the US was that after a very long flight we landed at Travis AFB and were told to fill out a customs form and then we would need to pass through a customs check. Before leaving the plane, I had kept an apple from my inflight meal thinking it would be nice to have later as a snack, nothing special about the apple, typical looking apple. As we filed through the customs shed in a single file, the agents pretty much just stamped papers and let everyone pass on through, until I got there that is. As I stood there with my sea bag on the table to be inspected, and my apple in my hand, the Customs Agent stared at me, then at the apple and then at me again. He said "You can't bring fruit into the country." He pointed to a trash barrel standing nearby. I threw the apple in the trash can and he stamped my papers and I went on through. Oh well, they didn't welcome me home, but they did take my apple.

While at home on leave the bad news came that a childhood friend, Steve Smith, US Marine Corps, had been killed in combat. I was able to be at the funeral before leaving for Mayport. It was a sad day with his mama dressed in black with a veil and the sharp looking Marines attending, the firing of the salute and playing of Taps making it an emotional moment especially when one of the Marines presented the folded flag, that had been draped over the casket, to his mother. He left behind a wife and baby. This moment had probably brought the war home to me more than my tour in county. And I didn't know yet that I had not seen the last of Vietnam.

Final Disposition of USS Jennings County

Severely damaged by an on-board fire in 1970 in the Mekong Delta

Decommissioned and struck from the Naval Register, 26 September 1970, at Naval Station Subic Bay, Republic of the Philippines

Sold for service as an ore barge for a mining company

Final Disposition, fate unknown

USS Jennings County *LST-846* earned one battle star for the Korean War and nine campaign stars for Vietnam War service

Sources for USS Jennings County information and photographs

Navsource.org

Warboats.org

Navyhistory.org

Various online sites

Déjà Vu
Aboard the USS Sphinx 1987

Many years after I left the Jennings County I would have a Deja Vu moment about the ship, It was in 1987 when I was acting Senior Chief of Command at Naval Station Panama Canal; the base had prepared a welcome for the USS SPHINX, an LST (later ARL-24) close to the same class as the Jennings County which had also served in the Riverine Force in Vietnam. It was Christmas time when she docked at Rodman Navy Base. She had spent long periods deployed offshore in the area and the base CO wanted to try to make their Christmas visit a nice one so we had a big welcoming crowd down at the pier to welcome the ship to the naval station. After it was tied up the base Captain was piped aboard for an official welcome to the ships Skipper who met us on the quarterdeck along with his Command Senior Chief, my counterpart.

We were escorted the wardroom, and I suddenly developed a weird feeling of stepping into the past as I walked along familiar passageways. It was the same identical layout as the Jennings County. The ship seemed smaller inside than I remembered; the overhead seemed closer, the passageways narrower. I did not ask to see the Radio Shack, things were moving too fast, and we were quickly back off the ship as there was a lot to do before evening as the ship's crew were being hosted at the various clubs that evening. I was almost glad as I was unprepared at how strong the flashback had come over me. Later I regretted not asking to visit the shack; it would have been a trip down memory lane for sure. At the Chief's club that night I spoke with the Skipper and when I told him about being aboard the Jennings County, he seemed to be a bit more interested in conversing with me than he had earlier. We spent a bit of time together before he departed for the Officer's Club.

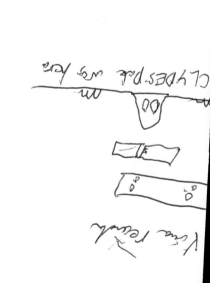

That would not be my only flash-back; another would happen to me during a cruise aboard the USS Forrestal some years later.

Next I was off to the USS Stribling DD-867, home ported at Mayport, Florida. AS I was leaving the JC the Stribling was prepping for its own trip to Vietnam though I didn't know this at the time. I left thinking I had seen the last of Vietnam.

From the brown water to the blue-water navy

USS Stribling DD-867

FORTUNE FAVORS THE BOLD

Flag Hoist/Radio Call Sign - **NBGI**

Tactical Voice Radio Call Sign (circa 1968) - **HOPE CHEST**

CLASS - GEARING As Built.
Displacement 3460 Tons (Full), Dimensions, 390' 6" x 40' 10" x 14' 4" (Max)
Armament 6 x 5"/38AA (3x2), 12 x 40mm AA, 11 x 20mm AA, 10 x 21" .(2x5).
Machinery, 60,000 SHP; General Electric Geared Turbines, 2 screws
Speed, 36.8 Knots, Range 4500 NM@ 20 Knots, Crew 336.
Operational and Building Data
Laid down by Bethlehem Steel, Staten Island NY January 15 1945.
Launched June 8 1945 and commissioned September 29 1945.
Completed FRAM upgrade May 1961.
Decommissioned and Stricken July 1 1976.
Fate Sunk as target off Puerto Rico July 27 1980.

Reporting Aboard
Mayport Florida

I reported aboard the USS Yellowstone, a destroyer tender, homeported in Mayport, to wait on the return of the USS Stribling, which at the time was undergoing refresher training in Guantanamo Bay, Cuba. By Coincidence my older brother Wayne was assigned aboard the Yellowstone working as a Mess Deck Master at Arms on the Galley mess deck, so we once again met up the last time being in Westpac. He knew the LPO for Radio and arranged for me to be assigned to the Radio Shack, so I wouldn't be stuck with Mickey Mouse duties, but I had to spend the first couple of days in the supply holds working until my clearance came through.

Not long after my arrival at Mayport my younger brother Donnie joined the Navy making all three of us brothers in the service at the same time. My brother Wayne and I went to see him before he flew out for boot camp he was staying at the same hotel in downtown Jacksonville that I had stayed at. He looked a little nervous about like I was before I left for Boot Camp. We probably didn't help ease his fear much but at least he got to see family before the craziness of basic training. In the end all three of us would serve in the Vietnam waters, Wayne on destroyers and Donnie on an aircraft carrier.

I also ran in to a few others I knew like my first Navy Chief, Chief Barnes, a brassy black boatswain mate Chief who had kept an eye out on me and kept me straight during my first year in the Navy. He is one I will never forget. He was on the quarterdeck of a Destroyer standing OOD and I spotted him as I was walking down the pier to the Yellowstone, or more accurately I heard him before I saw him as he had what you might call an attention getting voice that carried far, probably developed from years of yelling at stubborn seaman. We visited a few minutes on the quarterdeck before I went on my way. Another coincidental meeting was with the Master Chief of the Yellowstone who happened to have had the same role in Key West in my division, I can't recall his name, but he always looked like the ancient mariner, to me, or at least what I thought the ancient mariner looked like, old, gray haired and smoked a pipe. It was starting to feel like a Key West reunion I even tried to locate another sailor I knew who I found was a now a Third Class Boatswains Mate on yet another destroyer of the many moored in Mayport, but I was unable to get up with him before we deployed.

In just a few weeks the Stribling returned to Mayport, and that's when I found out she would be going to Vietnam on a Western Pacific Yankee Station cruise, departing in January 1969. So, I was headed back to Vietnam, and the hoped for easy, close to home, duty assignment I was looking forward to had gone down the pipe with that news. I was not happy and not looking forward to the cruise as it would be a long one, almost nine months. The ship would depart January 30, 1969 and return September 18, 1969.

The Stribling was a sleek looking war ship almost 180 degrees out in appearance from the Jennings County. The five-inch gun turrets were impressive, and she also had ASROC launchers which are rocket assisted torpedoes launched like a missile that were deployed as an anti-submarine weapon. My understanding of the theory behind these weapons was to launch a torpedo with a nuclear warhead far enough from the ship so the ship would survive though no one I ever discussed this with believed that would happen. If nothing else the concussion would crack open the hull and would sink the firing ship.

USS Stribling 1968

Nested outboard of the USS Yellowstone, Mayport

The USS Stribling was a WWII built destroyer launched too late in the war to participate in any action. She did however go on Westpac Cruise during the Korean conflict and provided support as an escort to various support ships so the Westpac cruise I would go on was not her first. She had several Mediterranean cruises chalked up, but this would be only her second Westpac.

Her history includes being commanded on her commissioning by Commander John D Buckley who had won the Medal of Honor for rescuing General Douglas MacArthur from the Philippines.

She was primarily deployed to the Mediterranean during her career, both before and after her 1969 Westpac cruise. Most of the following photos are from my Westpac Cruise book.

Westpac 1969

We departed Mayport on January 30, 1969 and I almost missed the departure. My girlfriend at the time had visited with her parents to see me off and we had gone out the night before. On the way back to Mayport their car broke down, in the middle of nowhere. We sat in the car all night until it was light enough to walk back down the road to a gas station where we bought a battery and the gas station owner drove us back to the car and helped install it. When I arrived at the base, the ship was just about ready to pull lines; I ran aboard and just made it and just in time to meet one of the other Radioman on the quarterdeck who was carrying a seabag which was mine, getting ready to take it off the ship. He told me to take the seabag back down to our berthing area and get up to radio to check in with the Chief.

I did so and was surprised that I was not chewed out as bad as I thought I would be, especially by RM1 Blackie the LPO. I guess he and the Chief had figured something like that had happened and was just glad I made it.

To back up a bit, when I went aboard the Stribling I was almost immediately assigned a watch section, no surprise there. I didn't require much of a break in since my year in Vietnam had made me fairly proficient on the watch standing routine and I knew all the standard equipment and one piece I really knew well was the first thing I saw when I entered radio, standing off to the left like a lone sentinel to the entry to radio, was my old nemesis the AN\URC-32 transceiver radio. I soon found out that it too, just like the one on the Jennings County, did not work and I knew that it would draw me in, at some point, into trying to get it to work at, but for now I had to learn the ropes of my new ship while underway. Back to good ole Port and Starboard watch standing.

Crossing the Pacific

Commanding the Stribling on the 1969 cruise was Commander William Costin an excellent skipper in my book and after serving on five ships, being stationed overseas three times and serving on a Surface Group Staff surrounded by high-ranking officers who had commanded at sea I still have him at the top of my list.

When we left for the Western Pacific and Vietnam, we took a route through the Panama Canal Zone, a place I would see more of later but did not know it at the time. Transiting the canal was interesting and when we reached the Pacific side and started up the coast, we made stops at Acapulco Mexico, San Diego and San Francisco before heading out to the Hawaiian Islands. We anchored at Pearl Harbor not far from the new Arizona Memorial which I could have visited but opted instead to take a bus tour of the Island with a bunch of crew members. We went to the Polynesian Village, which is still going in 2014 when I was there working as a military contractor. The tour was fun and interesting made numerous stops at other tourist spots. After the tour we all went to a bar and partied.

We loaded weapons in Pearl and headed west across the Pacific, making fueling stops I believe at Wake Island or may have been Midway before arriving at Subic Bay, in the Philippines. After a short refit there we left for Yankee Station where we would stay for 38 days before getting an R and R trip to Kaohsiung Taiwan and Hong Kong. Kaohsiung was not memorable, but Hong Kong Harbor was impressive, especially at night when thousands of lights were lit running up the hillsides around the harbor. I don't remember if we hit these ports before or after Yankee station.

Refueling in rough seas from the USS Chikaskia AO-54 in the Western Pacific I believe this is the 1969 cruise.

The trip across the Pacific was, and still is, my longest crossing and the Yankee Station cruise was my longest cruise of my Navy career.

The routine aboard ship for me, as a Radioman, while underway was to stand an eight-hour watch be off for eight and then back on. Known as Port and Starboard watch standing and it worked something like this. If you started a day shift at 7:30 AM, then you would be relieved at 3:30 PM. You would eat chow, maybe catch the movie then go to bed early because your next shift was at 11:30 PM for the mid watch. After your mid watch shift ended at 7:30 AM, you would eat breakfast and just to prove to you that you didn't need to go to sleep right away the off mid watch typically had to do compartment duties such as pick up and hand out laundry and field day the berthing compartment. When you did finally go to bed, or hit the rack as it was commonly referred to by sailors, it was never for as long as you would like as you had to be back on watch at 3:30 PM to start the Evening shift, or Eve watch, and this went on 24/7 and even when in port when the watches were split to fewer watch standers so three watch sections could be ran in order to provide a 2 out of 3 day liberty rotation. We still had to cover the entire 24 Hours, and the tempo was only slightly reduced during in port periods unless you had a message center ashore you could shift the message guard to. The US Navy bases like Yokosuka had such services and we could then just do message runs to pick up the daily traffic and the duty section would then distribute these messages. But even that was not a complete blessing as other maintenance work needed to be accomplished such as cleaning and doing preventive maintenance on antennas.

These port and starboard watches were called double back watches which allowed two sections to rotate so no one had the same shift all the time and all got to share in the misery of the different times of day. The Eve watch was always the busiest, this is when the officers are filing reports and supply is sending out supply messages. Then about 9 or 10 PM the HF frequency bands start to go to "Shits" (watch-standers term) meaning that atmospheric fluctuations and temperature changes played hell with the HF bands. During this period at least one Radioman had to continuously search the bands for stable and copyable broadcast frequencies that the Navy relied on for long hall communications. You may have a good frequency for just a few minutes when it will start to fade, this is when a good Radioman will already have another one set up on another radio that he will just patch over to so the message broadcasts are kept going and some of these technical control radioman could patch over radios so quickly they didn't lose crypto sync which could really sour a watch for everyone as you didn't want to miss any messages and chasing misser's (the task of re-scanning Teletype message traffic for missing message numbers) was a pain in the butt. To make matters worse, the in line crypto equipment had to be precisely in time and synced to the frequency or it wouldn't work so this added to the fun. The routine was tiring, but it did keep us busy and from being bored for sure. The mid-watches tended to slow down during the wee hours of the morning so there was time to read goof off with the bridge and CIC watches through the 1MC (or bitch box) the shipboard communications system.

Later the use of satellites for the broadcast made this hectic watch period a thing of the past.

One of the things I did early in the cruise was copy the UPI (United Press International) news Teletype frequency and print some of the more interesting stories on the duplicating machine, or ditto machine, which is way messier than a Xerox (which had not made their way in to the Stribling's radio shack yet). It used a purple based transfer sheet with a type of fluid called ditto fluid. After running off a few copies I would place some in the Wardroom and on the Mess deck for the officers and crew to read. I dropped this after we finished our trip across the Pacific and didn't restart it on the way back, I don't remember why I didn't.

The Battle group we were part of on the trip across held a contest amongst the ships for the crew member who had made the most Westpac Cruises. I didn't qualify for the Jennings County as it was not a Westpac Cruise but an in-country assignment. If I remember correctly, the winner was our ship with an older sailor, a Third-Class Petty Officer who had been on seven cruises. Why he was only a third class would probably be an interesting story if I knew it but I don't. He was called Pappy by the rest of the crew.

A cookout was thrown by the cooks on the helo-deck on a nice day while crossing; these are known in the Navy as Steel Beach days. The cooks did a great job, and we ate our fill of hamburgers and hot dogs.

Sundays were usually Holiday Routine, which means no work other than watch standing which is what most of us did for work, anyway. But they did show a movie on the mess deck in the afternoon and if you were off watch, you could watch that, and the Sunday meals were usually a little better than the normal fare, sometimes even steak.

Speaking of food, Navy chow is not bad, but it's also not elegant dining either and some stuff that's served regularly, like scalloped potatoes, become down right boring to eat. Milk becomes nonexistent after about a week underway, other than the powdered stuff, which I think should be outlawed, is a poor imitation of dirty water. Eggs went quickly also and became the powdered variety right along with the milk after the fresh ones were gone. I only ate powdered eggs one time in my twenty-five-year career and that was on the Jennings County and I never touched them again.

My favorite Navy meals were always spaghetti with spaghetti sauce and mashed potatoes with meat loaf. I always ate what was served, had to or starve, but I didn't always like what I ate.

In port the cooks had more to work with and the food variety increased, and we had plenty of milk and eggs, so a sailor soon forgot his underway food deprivations and enjoyed the bounty, till the next at sea time.

The Radio Shack

I don't recall all the names of the Radio Gang but there was a Chief Radioman who was wise enough to let the First-Class RM run things and RM1 Blackburn or "Blackie" ran the Radio Gang indeed and did a fine job of it too. Blackie could be firm and sometimes hard on you, but he also was a good teacher and would take time to talk to you like an older brother. I got along with Blackie very well.

There was RM3 "Buddy" Bruner who I would run in to again in Italy and RM3 Christian a very nice guy who worked in my section for a while. RM3 Jim "Mac" McKay was a fun loving guy. It was Jim that got me interested in Teletype repair showing me some things while standing watches. Later on I would attend Teletype Repair School in Norfolk, Virginia and would work as a Teletype repairman on the USS Forrestal. Another RM was RM3 Huffman. I would run in to Blackie, Bruner and Huffman again later on. RM3 Huffman would join the Naval Reserves and make Chief Petty Officer, I saw him while he was drilling when I was stationed at Newport Staff duty in 1989 or 1990. RM1 Blackburn I would run in to in Naples Italy and he would come over for Thanksgiving dinner while he was there. I also say Buddy Bruner in Naples.

It was a good radio gang from what I recall and we all got along with each other and outside the normal bickering and bitching typical of young men in a group we were like a family and like a family we would fight but would also stand up for one another.

LTJG Bob Warner was the Communications and Division Officer for the Radio Gang, he was a fine officer who seemed to care about his people. He administered my GED tests while we were on the cruise and his last words to me when I checked off the ship at the end of my enlistment was "I want you make use of those GED scores". I had failed one in math but made it up later. He was that type of person wishing well for others. I would love to be able to tell him I did make use of those GED scores and eventually earned a bachelor's Degree in History

LTJG BOB WARNER STRIBLINGS COMMUNICATIONS OFFICER WITH STRIBLING SKIPPER COMMANDER COSTON. I HAD A LOT OF RESPECT FOR BOTH OF THESE MEN.

Photo from www.ussstriblingdd867.org

The Radio Shack Layout as you entered in to central was a long compartment running in a bow to stern direction with equipment racks on the left and patch panels on the right. At the end of this compartment was a hatch leading in to the Radio Teletype and crypto compartment. Just before the entrance, on the right, was a small operator's desk with a typewriter and was primarily the supervisor's traffic checking position that the watch supervisor would use to check and route the daily messages to make sure they were delivered to the correct recipients for either action or information. The Radio Teletype room ran in port to starboard direction and was well packed with equipment and was a place that at least one watch stander, usually the junior person, would spend most of the watch, pulling messages off the Teletype, annotating with the routing and then running duplicate copies on a ditto machine.

There was a second area, outside and across a small passageway from Radio Central that was called the Radio Transmitter Room. It housed the two 500-watt transmitters that were used primarily for transmitting message traffic to shore Naval Communications Stations. These area NAVCOMMSTAS stations were located at different points around the world and kept the fleet in constant contact with the higher levels of command and with the Battle-group commander. The stream of traffic coming included messages for all the ships various departments, Supply, Engineering and Operations being the main three. Getting the traffic out and in was the Radio Gangs mission, and it was a tough one sometimes what the vagaries of the world's atmosphere which dictated the long-distance HF communications that was the method then in use.

No satellite communications were operational at the time but were on the planning board and would be a routine form of communications by the time I left the Navy many years later. But on the Stribling we fought the changing atmospherics, especially at night, almost constantly, never knowing when a good frequency would drop out and when it did it was quick, so you always had to be searching for another good one. The transmitters required a certain number of steps to tune up and sometimes you would have lost the frequency too bad propagation before you got back to central after tuning to try to send any message traffic.

WRT transmitters

*These are the type Radio transmitters that needed multiple
steps to tune requiring Radiomen to be quick about it before
frequencies shifted on them. Bragging rights went to the RM
who could tune the fastest with the least amount of SWR and
the tuning did not always follow the tuning instructions, there
are always shortcuts. The compartment these transmitters
were in was small and crowded with equipment but there was
enough room to squeeze in an ironing board to use for ironing
liberty whites.*

Yankee Station

Tonkin Gulf Vietnam

Yankee station was a point off Vietnam that had been used to launch aerial missions since about 1964, the early missions being photographic intelligence collection missions. With the escalation of the war it became the launch point for US Aircraft Carriers. The official designation was Point Yankee, but it was commonly referred to as Yankee Station, or by some more humorously by most sailors as the "Tonkin Gulf Yacht Club". It was this exclusive club that the USS Stribling Joined shortly after arriving following her long journey from Mayport, Florida.

We would spend a good bit of time cruising off the coast of Vietnam on Yankee Station in the Tonkin gulf. The only Vietnamese port we entered was Camh Rhan Bay, if I remember correctly, but maybe Danang harbor as well. But we mostly operated off shore providing gunfire support or plane guard for carriers and when relieved for R and R and refit we pulled in to another country's port, not any Nam ports.

For the most though it was either plane guard or gunfire support duties for the entire length of our stay on station. I sent out many a report regarding how much damage we did to Viet Cong supply dumps and casualties inflicted by our five-inch gun mounts, mainly all I heard all I heard was guns firing from either radio or berthing I was never outside when this went on so to me it was a lot of noise but no visual on what was happening. That was fine for gunfire support as it seemed to happen mostly at night and you don't want to be wandering around on a small ship in the dark with guns going off.

Next two photos from Stribling Cruise book.

Gunfire support in the Tonkin Gulf

First Stribling shell fired in combat in 24 years

"The first in twenty-four years."

Plane Guard
Plane Guard Duty, Tonkin Gulf Yankee Station

"You think he'll catch it?"

We also had interesting things happen at times, not war related, like when the laundry went out and we had to resort to washing our clothes by hand. Some would tie their dungaree pants to lines and drag them behind the boat in the salt water wash behind the propeller using it as an agitator, I didn't use this method preferring to do it in one of the small sinks in the head. The salt water tended to make the clothing rough, and I was afraid it would make me itch. There was laundry hanging all over the ships decks, probably wouldn't have presented a warlike picture to anyone observing us.

Laundry day on the bow under the watchful eyes of two 5-inch gun mounts that were on break from gunfire support. Photo is from the Stribling 1969 Cruise book

A Collision and Emergency Breakaway

We did have one big scare when an RVN tug towing a barge with garbage and no running lights passed through between us and an Oiler while refueling operations were underway at night. We had to do an emergency breakaway which spewed oil all over the side of the ship and the refueling crew on deck. The emergency break-away was initiated by the Stribling's Skipper after the oiler didn't act.

I was on mid watch when we hit the cable and was toppled out of the watch chair at the desk by the collision.

The cable the tug was using to pull the barge came across our bow and we hit it gouging a large rent in the bow. The tug passed between the oiler and the Stribling and how the crew managed to do the breakaway I still don't know. The next morning the Tug was standing off at anchor from us and the skipper sent over the only person on board who could speak French as most Vietnamese could speak that language from the years of French colonization of the country. I believe I remember hearing that the officer who went aboard soon radioed (to CIC or the bridge) back that the crew were not RVN but Pilipino. We had to break off operations and proceed to Kaohsiung for repairs after which we would return to the states.

My Communications Officer LTJG Bob Warner wrote a piece on the collision that I have included here. It provides some great detail on the event. It was posted on the ussstriblingDD867.org website.

The following item was copied from the USS Stribling website. Quoted in italics I did not include the pictures which can be viewed on the website.

The following pictures and comments have been

provided by Mr. Robert Warner who served as

Communications Officer in the late 60s

Collision while refueling from the USS Hassayampa off Da Nang about midnight. We were hooked up and fueling when our radar which showed an unknown contact with a good right bearing drift suddenly painted four contacts showing no lights with about 200 yards separation between each about 2,000 yards ahead. Captain Coston waited for less than a minute expecting the Senior CO on the oiler (in tactical command) to effect breakaway, and then, with no response from Hassayampa, took tactical command himself and ordered emergency breakaway. I think we used axes to cut through either the span wire or hoses and rolled heavily to starboard. Only seconds later we saw looming about 200 yards ahead one of the four contacts, a barge cabled apparently to other barges, invisible at night with no lights. The oiler cut through the cable between the last two barges, but we had nowhere to go and plowed into (I think) barge number 2. It put a big hole in our bow which the DCA, Ltjg Wright Nobel Rodman plugged with mattresses. Scared the piss out of me. Ltjg Wright Nobel Rodman, DCA.

Stuffed an 8' hole in the ships bow with mattresses after a collision with

unlit barge during re-fueling operation off Danang

Officer covered in oil after collision and emergency breakaway. Photo from Stribling 1969 Cruise book

Bow Repair

Repairs to damaged bow in Kaohsiung, Taiwan, looks like the repair patch is in place. Photo from www.ussstriblingdd867.org/ from crew member Ron Stokes posting.

Bow under repair alongside Tender in Kaohsiung. Ron Stokes photo posted on www.ussstriblingdd867.org/

Port Visits
Hong Kong River Junk Family (bottom)

When not on station the Stribling pulled into ports for upkeep, re-provisioning and crew liberty. Port visits were to Kaohsiung, Taiwan, Subic Bay, Hong Kong or Yokosuka with stops at San Francisco, Acapulco Mexico and Panama Canal Naval Station on the trips there and back from Mayport.

While in port in Hong Kong harbor and on one of my duty nights the weather had turned bad, other ships apparently were getting under way and the Skipper was asking about any message traffic regarding the Stribling getting under way. Nothing had come in addressed to us giving orders to sail early and I was sent by Whaleboat to check messages on other ships in the harbor for our missing messages after visiting two ships and finding nothing related to us getting underway I was brought back as the harbor was getting rough. We did get under way and I'm not sure under whose direction, but we got out of there ahead of the bad weather. I never knew why we didn't receive something telling us to get underway.

Prior to heading back across the Pacific towards home we pulled in to Kure Japan, the sister city of Mayport, Florida, and loaded a gift from Kure to haul back to their sister city of Mayport. The gift was a huge garden rock or maybe there were a couple; I don't recall. It rode on the fantail all the way across the Pacific as we went in reverse of our route over.

One other memory I have is visiting a ship, or what was left of it, at Subic Bay where we had stopped before heading back across the Pacific. The USS Evans had been hit by an Australian Aircraft Carrier while on station in the Tonkin Gulf and the stern half of the ship had been sheared off. I remember going by the dry dock it was located and seeing the ship. Seeing a destroyer, like the one you are on, with the bow section ripped off gives you a new perspective on the dangers of being a Tin-can sailor. Though we weren't in the area where the accident happened there had been plenty of message traffic on this, so I was curious to see it. I don't recall who was with me but I some of us visited what was left of the Evans in Subic.

There has been an ongoing effort by surviving crew of the Evans and other veterans to have the names of the 74 sailors killed during the collision added to the Vietnam Wall memorial. As far as I know this has not happened up to the time of this writing. In my opinion if a U.S. military service member is killed during operations in a combat zone, whether by a friendly or an enemy, you're still dead because of the war and this should be acknowledged as a combat death.

A Radioman Second Class was one of the 74 that died.

USS Evans stern section the bow was torn off in a collision with the HMS Melbourne (Navsource)

Photo # NH 98651   USS Everett F. Larson alongside the after section of USS Frank E. Evans

Return to Mayport

Before our return trip, when we were still in the Pacific, the skipper, Commander Coston, had requested an around the world route back to the Mayport but it was denied, I was thankful in a way as I didn't want to go through the shellback initiation; I remained a Pollywog all my 25-year Navy career.

Nothing much exciting on the return trip, other than it seemed to take forever. In Pearl Harbor at the Enlisted Club I ran in to a hometown guy that I knew from site but not personally, he was younger than me but recognized me and called out to me from another table and we talked for a bit. The show that night was a fellow by the name of Jimmie Rodgers, he sang a late 1950s pop hit song called Honey Comb and I really enjoyed the show.

We made our last port call before arriving back at Mayport in Key West, Florida, my first duty assignment. I walked down to the pier area after returning from liberty, the place where I had worked when stationed there, and found the small boat I was assigned to and was looking it over thinking of all the days I spent chipping paint and painting in the hot Key West sun when a guard came by and, though friendly enough, advised me I was not allowed on the pier at night. He was standing the same pier watch I used to stand on my duty nights.

Manning the rails in dress whites for the arrival in

On pulling in to Mayport as we came in through the breakwater channel some sailors who were soon to be separated from the service did what was a Navy tradition of throwing your hat in to the water signifying this was your last cruise. I didn't throw mine in even though I had determined to separate, guess I wasn't totally convinced it would be my last cruise and it wound up to not be.

We still had the Kure garden rocks and the supply officer had sent the usual message asking for port services and the last item was for a crane to help the Stribling get her rocks off. I thought that was funny. It had been a long cruise, and I was glad it was ending, and we were finally home.

Déjà vu all over again
Aboard a Greek Destroyer Off Sicily 1974

Years later when I was serving on board the USS Forrestal, CVA-59 during a Mediterranean Cruise and assigned to and working in the Teletype Repair shop as a Teletype repairman we were anchored off Sicily with our Battle-group and I was on duty that day. My Chief called over and said I was needed to assist a Greek destroyer with a broken Teletype. I was taken over on the ships liberty boat, lugging my tool kit along since I didn't know what they would have, and when I boarded the ship Greek sailors escorted me to the RadioShack and wow did I have a flashback as I stepped through the door into Radio, I knew the Greek Destroyer was similar to the Stribling but until I set foot in the Shack; I hadn't realized it was a sister ship with the exact same layout as the USS Stribling, even to the worn looking supervisors watch desk in Radio Central, it was enough to make me dizzy for a second.

The Shack had no air conditioning and whether it was broken or just not turned on who knows, and I didn't ask but it was hot. The Greeks showed me what was wrong with the Teletype and boy it was in bad shape. I had enough experience in Teletype repair by now to recognize that this machine was in such sad shape that it would need more than I could do to get it back to 100 percent; it needed a complete overhaul or rebuild.

I did my best and got it workable but with problems still extent and I had to stop as the Forrestal was calling for my return since we would be sailing soon. I explained to the Greek Radioman that it would need an overhaul to bring it back to good condition, so they offered me a cup of cold coffee which I drank and didn't like much then said goodbye to the Greek sailors and headed back to the Forrestal.

Vietnam battle awards, decommissioning and disposal

The USS Stribling earned two battle stars during the Vietnam War; according to the Navy Unit Awards posted on awards.navy.mil she also earned credit for the Armed Forces Expeditionary Medal for the periods 17 to 23 July 1958; 25 June 1968; and 9 to 15 June 1969. Credit for Vietnam Service was accrued during the periods 20 March 1969 to 25 April 1969; 4 to 26 May 1969; 28 June 1969 to 2 July 1969; and 12 July 1969 to 3 August 1969. The Stribling also earned credit for the Republic of Vietnam Gallantry Cross Unit Citation with Palm during the periods 21 March 1969 to 2 April 1969; and 23 to 26 July 1969.

THE USS STRIBLING WAS DECOMMISSIONED AND STRICKEN FROM THE NAVAL VESSEL REGISTER ON 1 JULY 1976. SHE WAS SUNK AS A TARGET ON 27 JULY 1980

USS Stribling Anchor on display at Mays Landing, NJ VFW

About the Author

Tom Johnson is a retired US Navy Senior Chief Radioman (SW) transferring to the Fleet Reserve on May 30th, 1990 after 25 years of service and transferring to the permanent retired list in May 1995. His duty stations during those 25 years were:

1965-66

Basic Training Great Lakes

Key West Test and Evaluation Detachment Key West, FL

1967-1968

Radioman Class A School.

USS Jennings County LST-846, Republic of Vietnam

1968-1969

USS Stribling DD-867, Mayport, Florida

1970-1973

Comfairmed Naples, Italy

Naval Communications Station Naples, Italy

1973

Radioman Class B School, Sand Diego, CA

1974

Teletype Repair School,, Norfolk, VA.

1974-1976

USS Forrestal CVA-59, Norfolk, VA.

1976-1977

USS Leahy CG-16, Norfolk, VA, and San Diego, CA

1977-1981

Naval Radio Receiving Facility Kamiseya, Japan

1981-1984

USS Patterson FF-1061, Mayport, FL

1984-1987

Naval Station Panama Canal, Rodman and Fort Amador

1987-1990

Commander, Naval Surface Group Four, Newport, RI.

1990 Transfer to Fleet Reserve

1990 Transfer to permanent Retired List.

Manufactured by Amazon.ca
Bolton, ON